NEW WINGS FOR WOMEN

Sally Knapp

In these days when we are striving toward "One World," the modern airplane is the mechanical means for making this possible. In the years to come, flights to China, the Soviet Union, and South Africa will seem as commonplace as a drive from New York to Boston today, and probably won't take much longer. The pioneers of flight—the Wright Brothers, Charles Lindbergh, Eddie Rickenbacker—are well known to even the least air-minded layman, but the women who have had to battle on two fronts are not so well known. They have worked not only for the advancement of aviation, but also for the right of women to make their way in a so-called man's field.

New Wings for Women is a group of biographies of women of spirit and initiative who have stepped into the magic aeronautical circle drawn by men, to pave a way for women in aviation tomorrow. It fuses the human story of the women themselves with an over-all picture of the work they are doing in many different branches of aviation.

We meet Pauline Gower of Britain, Helen Harrison of Canada, Valentina Grizodubova of Russia, as well as many Americans, for women in each of these countries have made unique and outstanding contributions to aviation. Women test pilots, meteorologists, aircraft designers, flight nurses, and aeronautical engineers have opened the doors to a wealth of interesting, exciting jobs for women. They laughed at the idea that women are fitted only for manipulating a frying pan or vacuum cleaner, and showed they are just as capable with a monkey wrench, T-square or "joy stick."

These are the leaders today for women in aviation tomorrow.

(120-160)

New Wings for Women

SALLY KNAPP

Thomas Y. Crowell Company
NEW YORK

To my friend,

OLIVE BADEAU

with gratitude for "mechanical help"—and so much more.

PREFACE

YOUR grandchildren will look back upon three distinct eras in aviation for women.

The first, in aviation's infancy between two World Wars, was an age of stunt flyers and record-breakers. If a girl achieved anything in aviation in those days except by marrying a pilot, or by interesting some wealthy promoter in her ambitions, she was a very rare product indeed.

The second era, ushered in by the threat of the Second World War, was very different. A million girls in hundreds of aviation jobs chiseled away the wall of prejudice, block by block. So today, as we enter the third era, just about every door in the aviation industry is open to women.

The personalities introduced to you in this book represent the second era. In the long ledger of service and achievement in many fields, made by the women of Allied countries during the past war, the progress of women in aviation stands out in boldfaced type.

As flight instructor for the W.A.S.P. (Women's Airforce Service Pilots) and aviation writer, I have been fortunate in knowing many of these women personally. Others I have met indirectly through the airport grapevine so well known to anyone who flies.

During the years that England, Russia, Canada,

China, and the United States fought together against a common enemy, these women conquered new fields in aviation or climbed to higher pinnacles in the old. Aviation is a universal language and, whatever their differences in race, creed, political doctrine, or nationality, all were united by a love of flying and a fight for freedom.

Those who are in high-school preflight classes, college flying clubs, and Wing Scout troops today will widen the fields these women have pioneered. Tomorrow they will create the third era for women in aviation. Their role will be less spectacular perhaps, but more secure, for behind them stand nearly thirty-five years of accomplishment, a continuous history of women overcoming handicaps. What these women have done, their successors can do—and a great deal more!

Sally Knapp

CONTENTS

New Wings for Women

TEDDY KENYON

"THERE's a stiff wind blowing today—forty or fifty miles, I'd say," one of Grumman's veteran pilots spoke up, as a dozen men and three girls, test pilots all, lounged about the "ready room," waiting for their assigned flights to be chalked up on the board.

"Did anyone ever tell you how to land if you have to jump in a high wind like this?" he continued to the pilot nearest him, a slight, blue-eyed girl adjusting a helmet over her long light-brown bob. "You just unbuckle your harness as you near the ground, keeping your arms crossed over your chest to hold the chute on until just before you touch the ground, then throw your arms out and slide through. That way you won't be dragged along the ground."

"Thanks a lot," Teddy smiled at him, "I may need to know that some time!" And she picked up her parachute and headed for the flight line where a mechanic was warming up the Navy Hellcat she was to take on its test hop.

Its nose pointed into the wind, the Hellcat rose from the runway, in a swelling crescendo of sound. At two hundred feet it would make a 90 degree left turn, following the airport traffic pattern. But it didn't—it climbed straight ahead, one mile up into the blue.

Something was definitely wrong! The old pilot's words were ringing in her ears. It looked as if she might have immediate use for her new knowledge.

In the closed cockpit cold sweat stood out on Teddy's forehead as she climbed steadily upward, caught in a pilot's nightmare—jammed controls! They had worked all right before she took off. Eleven thousand pounds of powerful fighter plane in which your first mistake might well be your last—and the stick refused to move beyond dead center to the left!

At six thousand feet she drew a deep breath. Now at least the most valuable asset any pilot in trouble can have was hers—six thousand wonderful feet of altitude in which to think.

She tried the stick again, experimenting; it worked to the right but not to the left. Strange! She pulled up the floor covering, but could find nothing wrong when she bent down to look in. She even kicked the stick, but it wouldn't budge an inch.

"This is it!" she thought. "Here's where I hit the silk!" And the old pilot's instructions raced through her mind.

Time to let the radio tower back at the field know what was happening: "I have a jammed aileron, can't move the stick to the left—don't know what causes it," she called in.

Connie, the chief pilot, made three steps at a time going up to the tower. His soothing voice suggested several possible remedies for the situation, and Teddy tried them all. Nothing helped, so Connie said: "Drop your flaps and wheels to be sure they're working O.K."; then, "See if you can pick up the left wing with the rudder if necessary, slowed up, as you would be for a landing."

And finally the all-important question: "How do you feel about bringing her in—would you rather bail out?"

What a decision to have to make—to risk her neck in a lopsided landing that might well end in a crack-up, if a sudden gust of wind hit the crippled wing—or to bail out and let $90,000 worth of airplane go smash! Teddy decided to try for a landing.

"The field is clear, come on in!" Connie's voice came through. Teddy circled down in wide right-hand spirals. It seemed as if everyone at the Grumman Aircraft Plant were out on the field, helping her down. Fire engines, ambulances, and men in asbestos suits stood by.

"Just in case a gust of wind hits that left wing and I can't pick it up quickly enough, so we spin in and maybe catch fire," Teddy thought grimly, watching the group below, but she was too busy landing the plane to give more than a passing thought to this possibility.

The ground rushed up to meet her. The left wing dropped momentarily and every heart stopped beating. She picked it up quickly by using the rudder and an audible sigh ran through the crowd—watching, waiting.

The Hellcat touched the ground in a perfect landing, and as a tired girl stepped out of the cockpit onto the wing, an anxious masculine voice inquired: "Are you all right, Honey?"

Teddy pulled her helmet off and grinned down at her husband and the others who had rushed out to the ship. "Thank goodness, I made a decent landing with swooped low over excited crowds, or climbing from a speeding car up a shaky rope ladder into the plane precariously balanced in flight by his partner.

One day Ted met an old friend who had just bought an OX Travelair which needed some work done on its throttle. Ted fixed it in his shop, and the friend said, gratefully: "As soon as I solo this ship, I'll check you out in it."

That's the way they did things in the early days of flying—anyone with an hour's solo time was a self-appointed instructor. With two hours solo in the OX to his credit, Ted took Teddy up, zoomed over her home in Connecticut, picked a smooth field to land in, taxied the ship up under a tree, and went in to visit her family.

The owner of the Travelair left his ship with the Kenyons for the summer while he was away, and in the fall they bought the plane from him.

One Sunday, after a particularly good day in which Ted had picked up a few hundred dollars just flying from field to field, giving rides, he said to Teddy: "Gosh, Honey, maybe we're in the wrong business!" So he and two college students started a company.

Each of his partners also contributed a plane to the company, and the first summer that they were in business the company grossed $17,000. However, success went to the heads of Ted's two partners, and they soon were completely out of hand. So Ted brought his brief barnstorming career to an end.

The Kenyons bought an Arrow Sport, a small side-by-side airplane with dual controls, and Ted taught Teddy to fly in a few hours. Ted assures us that this was because she was an exceptional student, but Teddy denies it, saying it was all due to his fine instruction. Soon she was tossing the small plane around the sky in many extraordinary and often quite original maneuvers.

Ted was now flying for Colonial Airlines, and Teddy flew with him whenever possible, often piloting the plane when there were no passengers aboard. Teddy spent most of her flying time during the next three years, however, participating in air meets up and down the east coast. In aviation's early days these meets were held frequently throughout the countrty to promote public interest in flying. The public wanted stunts and races and record-breaking flights—so, for women flyers in particular, these meets provided just about the only real contribution to aviation they could make at the time.

Ted watched his wife fly whenever he could; and, every time she came down, he went over every move she had made, drawing diagrams and explaining how she could improve her technique. This was exactly what she wanted, for Teddy Kenyon is the kind of person who never stops learning. She would be the first one to admit that Ted has been largely responsible for her success as a pilot, by teaching her, encouraging her, and working with her.

In 1930 the American Legion in Boston offered a $300 cash prize for an unusual aerial contest in which the pilot's appearance and manner were considered as well as flying ability. Teddy's flying was superb, and her smiling poise and charming appearance did the rest—she came home triumphantly with the prize.

Ted was not impressed. "Fine, Dear, but now I'm sure you want to fly in earnest," was all he said.

Teddy did begin flying in earnest. Her greatest satisfaction in flying has always been to assist her husband in his development of new instruments and simplified blind-flying devices. Now he bought a Waco and it was Teddy's job, as Ted ironed out some new wrinkle in one of his inventions and installed it in the plane, to fly through a series of maneuvers which would test the efficiency of the new device.

Whether working on intricate calculations in the shop they have built in their home, or skimming the skies together, these two share a basic job—and a mutual trait of character—to do something well and then learn to do it better.

Now and then Teddy still took part in an air meet or competition in her locality. In 1933 a Civil Aeronautics contest was held to determine the national sportsmen's champion. Thirty-nine men and women entered to compete for the honor and the $5000 cash prize. The tests were not dangerous or extraordinary but required a high degree of skill and had to be well practiced before hand.

Teddy decided that she would like to enter this contest, but Ted very practically asked: "And what will you use for a plane?" A ship with higher performance than the one they owned was absolutely essential if she was to have any chance at all.

Teddy soon solved this problem by approaching the owner of a Waco biplane at the local airport with this proposition: "If you will lend me your plane to practice for this competition, I'll give you $1000 if I win, otherwise I'll just pay you for the use of the ship, gas and oil—at the usual rates."

This bargain agreed upon, Teddy went to work, per-

fecting her technique for the big event. Every day for
the two weeks preceding the conference she practiced
spot landings, until she was able to set the Waco down
within a few feet of the mark. Then she began to practice stunts. There wasn't much time to perfect these
maneuvers, and practices were few and far between because, after all, the owner of the plane needed it to
make a living. Teddy had to squeeze in practice time
when he wasn't flying.

The big event finally arrived. One by one the contestants were eliminated until only two women and
two men remained after two days of gruelling competition. Teddy was one of them. At the end of the second day, the Waco's owner, hearing that his "dark
horse" was doing so well, hurried down from Boston
to give Teddy instruction in Immelmann turns. The
morning before the final competition he and Teddy
did fifteen consecutive Immelmanns—the long dive,
the start of the loop, the snap and outward thrust as the
ship rolled over. It was hard work.

Thousands of people watched the final trial. Teddy's small biplane started its dive into the first half of
the Immelmann loop, its engine whining and spurting
misty gasoline. The plane righted itself and climbed
skyward again, to repeat the maneuver. Three perfect
Immelmanns in a row, and the crowd broke into a
cheer as the plane's wheels touched the ground a few
minutes later in a perfect landing. Teddy, tired but
elated, climbed out of the plane and stepped forward
to receive the silver trophy, cash award, and title of
"sportsman champion."

By the next morning, Teddy had paid her debt to
the owner of the Waco, bought a car, a new airplane,

and three suits for her husband. She arrived home penniless but happy.

Her flying skill had been judged excellent by experts, so Ted had no reason to hesitate in asking her to assist him in the work he was doing for the Sperry Gyroscope Company. He had invented a blind flying instrument, called a deviometer, some time before. Since this had been in direct competition with products of the Sperry company, they had bought out the company that he had formed and asked Ted to come and work for them. Teddy became his copilot. She did many of the experimental flights and also took up company officials to observe the instruments in flight. In fact, it was Teddy who flew to Wright Field at Dayton to demonstrate their new automatic pilot to army officials.

As soon as war was declared, Teddy, like many other civilian pilots, started flying with the Civil Air Patrol, but before long she was doing a much more vital war job. Ted had been making business trips to Grumman Aircraft Corporation at Farmingdale for some time. One day he told Teddy: "They need pilots at Grumman to pick up small parts and instruments from other plants which are needed at the home plant and can't wait for regular delivery. Why don't you volunteer for the job?"

"One day," Teddy said, "I was at Grumman when no man was available and they needed parts from another plant right away, so Bud Gillies, vice-president of Grumman, an old friend of ours, said, 'You go get them, Toots!' and I did."

After this had happened several times more, Bud announced one day: "As of November 1, you are on the

Grumman payroll." And for the next few months Teddy continued to make trips in Grumman's Fairchild plane to Hartford, Kingston, Boston, Philadelphia, to get whatever parts were needed.

Before long Bud was saying: "You'd better get a commercial license." So Teddy started to study. It's hard work to get back to the routine of studying when you've been out of school for quite a few years, especially if you are doing it on your own, without benefit of regular classes. Teddy was afraid she'd never make it, but she passed the examination without too much difficulty.

"Now," said Bud, "go get an instrument rating." And Teddy did.

Ted joined Grumman the following January and went to work on a new maneuvering automatic pilot. Teddy by now was flying amphibious twin-engine Widgeons for the company, and twin-engined JRF's with 900 horsepower. Pilots say, "If you can fly these JRF's, you can fly anything! Overloaded and not very pleasant to fly, they are regular aerial trucks." Teddy adds: "With the gliding angle of a streamlined brick."

But these very unattractive characteristics of the JRF's proved to be disguised blessings for Teddy and the other two girls, who by now had been added to the Grumman staff, Barbara "Kibby" Jayne and Lib Hooker. JRF's made checking out in other type aircraft easy by comparison.

Teddy had always wanted to fly a fighter but thought it an impossible dream until one day Bud, with typical nonchalance, announced: "I think this would be a good day to check you girls out on Hellcats."

Behind every story of an unusual opportunity for

women you will find some man who believed in them and gave them a chance to prove what they could do. Bud Gillies had faith in these three girls and he believed that competent women pilots did a fine job of selling aviation to the public.

Teddy was scheduled to go upstate on a delivery trip for the company and all day the fear haunted her that Bud might not wait until she returned in the evening to make the flights. But she crossed her fingers, took the Hellcat instruction book with her, and read it from cover to cover en route upstate.

Much to her relief, Bud had waited; and, almost as soon as she returned, he said to the girls: "The three ships are O.K. You want to go up in them?"

Teddy had sat in the ship just once and had been shown the instruments—that was all. Now she was expected to take this hot ship up by herself and bring it down safely. Bud gave her one final word: "Don't let it fly you. Remember, there's a lot of weight there!"

Vice-president Gillies had really stuck his neck out this time. Here were three girls who had never before flown fighter ships, taking up $375,000 worth of airplanes solely on his authority.

Teddy couldn't believe her luck. Once she was off the ground and climbing straight up, she pinched herself, and then again, just to make sure. "It was like music, that take-off—the roar of the engine as the ship gathered speed, ending in a high screaming crescendo of sound as I closed the hatch. I remember thinking, 'Now what in heck is the matter with that altimeter?' I never had climbed so fast. In mid-air I let the flaps and landing wheels down just to see how they felt. As I throttled back and started to glide earthward, I was thinking, like any pilot in a new plane, 'After all it's the landing that counts!' "

It was a good landing and on succeeding days there were more check-outs in Hellcats and in torpedo-bomber Avengers. A month after the first Hellcat flight, the girls were told: "O.K., now you can do production tests on Hellcats as often and as many as you like in a day."

Every Hellcat had to have one hour and five minutes check time in the air before being turned over to the Navy. Each girl made from four to six flights a day of about forty-five minutes each, with a complicated check list in hand to check for minor adjustments that had to be made. Occasionally the plane would be nearly perfect and then they would finish out the sixty-five minutes on the first flight.

Flight testing new planes is hard and extremely tiring work. This constant up and down, in and out of planes all day is much more wearing than straight flying. Men flying for Grumman who had been flying ten hours a day, six days a week on cross-country ferrying jobs, found that they couldn't take much of this. There is a large element of nervous strain in these flights for, after all, these are new ships just off the production line and anything can happen!

If you think flying, half frozen in winter in sub-zero temperatures, or grinding dust between your teeth under the glare of the hot summer sun, is a glamorous job, just ask Lib, or Kibby, or Teddy. Talking to them, you'd soon get rid of any notion that it's romantic and dashing to be a flyer. These girls are no daredevils, just three pilots doing an exacting job. Somehow a flyer, and a woman test pilot particularly, doesn't do much crowing—it might be her last crow if she got too cocky.

"We certainly have about as different backgrounds as three gals doing the same job could possibly have," Teddy said. "Lib started to be a doctor but decided she liked flying better, and Kibby is married to a Navy flyer, who most appropriately flies Hellcats. Incidentally, these were the Navy's newest fighters when we started testing them, and they were knocking down Jap Zeros in the Pacific at a ratio of about twenty to one."

Meeting Teddy Kenyon on the street, you'd never guess that her chief occupation is flying hot fighter planes at 250 knots speed on their test flights, nor that beneath her gay, friendly, smiling exterior lies not only a fine pilot but also a student of navigation and an excellent mechanic.

She can't say enough in praise of the Hellcat: "It's such a beautiful ship that any two-year-old could fly one—so why all the fuss?" is the way she sums it up. "It's really a pilot's delight and I marvel contsantly that a plane of such high performance could be so easy to fly."

"The only real excitement we had testing these planes," Teddy continued, grinning, "was the day Lib bailed out. I was returning from a test flight at the time, and just took in the situation in snatches over the radio. It seems her motor started quitting over Connecticut; and, muttering 'This can't happen to me,' she called in, giving the tower her position—and then added that the flames were beginning to creep up through the floor and she thought it was time for her to leave.

"Lib rode that Hellcat down to fifteen hundred feet

so that it would land in the Sound instead of in some unsuspecting citizen's back yard, and then went over the side. She said later that she never had seen a more beautiful sight in her life than that white canopy billowing above her. On the way down she saw the plane explode as it landed in a swamp, and she felt much better about it, knowing it had landed clear of any buildings or people.

"By this time I had landed at the field and, with everyone else, was waiting anxiously for some further word. Lib meanwhile had landed in someone's back yard, she told us later, where she must have scared the lady of the house half to death by appearing in a grease-streaked flying suit with a parachute harness over her shoulder and inquiring, 'May I use your telephone?' I guess the lady thought the Mars invasion had finally come!

"We received the call at the field five minutes after Lib had bailed out—the longest five minutes I've ever known."

That night they all went to a party, Lib just as calm as if she bailed out of a plane every day.

These girls feel their responsibilities very keenly and they take a real interest in turning out the best planes possible, not just ones that are "good enough." It's not how many planes they can check out and deliver, it's how nearly perfect they can make each one.

There are a dozen small things that may be wrong with any new plane, just tiny adjustments that may mean the difference between life and death for some Navy flyer over the Pacific. For instance, that session with the jammed controls that Teddy had. The whole difficulty was caused by the failure of one small pin which allowed a rod to drop and jam the aileron control. Every once in a while something does happen on one of these production tests, otherwise there would be no purpose in testing.

Ted said: "I think this exactness that is characteristic of Lib, and Kibby, and Teddy is due to the fact that they could see a step beyond the test flight and visualize the man who would fly it in combat. They could picture some poor devil with a Zero on his tail, and the best was not good enough."

Teddy added: "Individual planes vary a great deal; that is one reason they have to be test-flown. Why one is so much better than another when all go through the same mill no one knows, but they are. Some are delightful to fly and the test pilot says: 'Boy, I wish this baby were mine!' And others they wouldn't take as a gift! That's our job, to iron out these little differences and try to make them all as good as the best one.

"Planes do have definite personalities. Some just don't click and you can't put your finger on what is wrong, but the funny thing is, every pilot who flies it has the same idea about the same plane."

Teddy is a supersalesman for aviation, and for women in aviation in particular. You've never met a woman so enthusiastically interested in helping other women pilots, or so anxious to give any one of them a break whenever possible. Why every girl doesn't fly is a mystery to her.

"A girl can handle a plane with as much precision as a man. It doesn't take muscle," she says. "Flying gives you a wholly different perspective on life, a sort of spiritual something that makes you feel good inside.

It's strange but all pilots feel that way, though some of them won't admit it."

As a charter member of the 99's, the national women flyers organization, Teddy feels a keen concern for the future of women pilots in aviation as a profession. "I think there will be some jobs for women pilots in the future, as instructors, test pilots (especially in companies manufacturing smaller aircraft), and in miscellaneous commercial jobs, such as selling ships to the public and air-cargo transportation. In fact, it seems to me that the only flying job not open to women yet is on the major airlines. This is not because they lack any ability as pilots but because public opinion has so far not been educated to this point.

"It is hard to say just what the opportunities for women pilots will be with so many men now returning from the air forces, but I think there will always be some flying jobs open to top-notch women. Of course, as in many other professions, they will have to be better qualified than men applying for the same job to get it."

The greatest contribution of women pilots to postwar aviation will undoubtedly be as sportsmen pilots. There is a big job of promoting air-mindedness among American women to be done, and these ex-WASP's, ex-instructors, and ex–test pilots are the ones to do it.

Teddy added: "I don't know that I'll continue testing Hellcats now that the war is over, but I'll always fly. Those of us who love this game will keep flying as long as we can move a muscle."

And as a final thought: "A young couple can get a great deal of fun out of flying together. Look at Ted and me!" And one look would convince you that there couldn't be a happier pair. The Kenyons have truly made their mutual interest in flying the magic carpet to a happy marriage.

PAULINE GOWER

EVERY American girl who today earns a sportsman's pilot's license, or makes flying her career, without encountering mountains of prejudice and discrimination owes a tremendous debt to a small group of English girls. By their fine record they broke down prejudice and established the right of women pilots to be judged by their skill alone.

To a large extent all owe their opportunities to one farsighted woman pilot—Commander Pauline Gower of Britain.

In a small, square office, among the camouflaged hangars and workshops of a busy British airdrome, a quiet, gray-eyed woman, with three gold shoulder bars on her trim navy-blue uniform, sat at her desk, efficiently directing the activities of more than a hundred top-notch women pilots. These women had been gathered from half a dozen Allied countries to ferry British planes from factories to fighter bases all over the country.

Out on the field, military planes in their dull war paint came and went on urgent business. Spitfires zoomed overhead and Wellington bombers shook the walls of the small office, drowning out parts of the conversation.

"You are to start in twenty minutes to take an Oxford to ——" came the order, in a quiet, authorative voice, and the girl scheduled for the job set out to fly the twin-engined bomber to the other end of the country with as little fuss as though she were driving her convertible into town.

A tired, dust-streaked young woman in greasy flying suit, with a parachute swung wearily over one shoulder, entered the office to report to the director of women personnel that she had just brought a badly crippled Lancaster safely home to the field.

As Britain's foremost woman in aviation, the only one ever to attain the rank of commander, Pauline Gower organized the world's first group of women ferry pilots before England had been at war six months. Her headquarters were as modest and unostentatious as Pauline herself. On the walls of the office were pictures of military aircraft and a winged lion which had been cut out and pasted there, with its paw resting on a map of Britain. A chart hanging behind her desk showed the position of every woman pilot in the A.T.A. and the particular flying job she was on at the moment. The businesslike austerity of the desk with its neat pile of official documents and portable typewriter was offset by a bowl of moss, filled with violets and snowdrops.

Pauline Gower wouldn't take no for an answer. As soon as the Air Transport Auxiliary was formed to give men pilots, who for some reason could not qualify for the R.A.F., an opportunity to serve their country, she began worrying the Air Ministry. They reluctantly consented to allow her, with a hand-picked group of eight more women pilots, to prove, if she could, that competent women flyers had a real contribution to make to the air war too.

She doesn't like to talk about herself, typical British reticence you might say, but a warm smile lights up her face and a look of great pride shows in her eyes when she talks about her girls.

One look at the record would convince you that her pride is justified. Now that the war is over, it may be possible to compute what the A.T.A. meant to the R.A.F. in saving of time and personnel. In the first two years of the war alone, men and women of the A.T.A. flew 30 million miles and delivered 100,000 planes from factory to unit bases. Pauline Gower's group of women pilots made up about one-fourth of the total A.T.A.

"We certainly have learned one thing from this experience of working side by side with Commander Gower's group," said one A.T.A. commander at the end of the war—"that women fly as neatly and precisely as men—and with greater safety."

But as always when women have made a break into a so-called "man's world," the nine women in the first experimental group had considerable prejudice to break down during that first winter of the war. And what an experience that was! For seven months they safely delivered to various flight bases every small training ship assigned to them, without even bending a blade of grass.

Not one of them will ever forget the pain of thawing out, after ferrying open-cockpit, unprotected Tiger Moths, throughout the country in temperatures of 25 and 30 below zero. They could not have been given a more severe test. Also, after they landed they usually had to lug parachutes in the bitter cold another mile or two to the nearest billet, because there were no sleeping quarters or accommodations of any kind for women at the base. But they plugged away, confident that in time their ability would be recognized.

And it was, for in the spring Pauline was asked by the Air Ministry to double her numbers immediately; and by January, 1942, more than a hundred hand-picked women pilots were ferrying all the 120 different types of aircraft flown by the A.T.A., even the heaviest four-engined bombers.

Despite this exceptional record, such phrases as "heroines of the air" set Pauline's teeth on edge. She detests glamorization of women's work and, in fact, all kinds of overstatement.

"This was one of the chief reasons for the barrier of prejudice erected against women pilots in the beginning," she said. "Let's not talk about heroines of the air! Flying is a job, and like any other should be done by the people qualified to do it. Women in this service were treated exactly like the men, that's one of the things I fought for from the beginning. I have no patience with the type of girl who asks for equal treatment with men, and then, when she gets it, expects special consideration because she is a woman.

"At this airdrome there were men and women ferry pilots, R.A.F. cadets in the school, pilots of all kinds taking refresher courses on new types of ships, and both men and women flight instructors. It was purely a question of ability and the person best qualified to do a particular job was the one who did it."

Only long personal experience as a pilot could have qualified Pauline Gower for her position, no matter how much administrative ability she possessed. An active flyer since nineteen, she was no mere "arm chair" officer.

When Pauline was born in Kent, England, in 1910, her father, Sir Robert Gower, now a member of Parliament, was a solicitor and her mother a brilliant musician. Fortunately for Pauline, she inherited both her father's executive talents and her mother's musical gift. The ways in which girls have financed their flying lessons are many and varied, but it is doubtful if any other girl has paid for her flight instruction by giving violin recitals, as Pauline Gower did.

After she and her sister had completed their education at a convent school in England and a finishing school in Paris, Pauline told her father that she wanted to learn to fly. With a horrified "No," he refused point-blank to give her any money for "such foolishness," so Pauline turned to her one real earning power and literally "fiddled" her way into a "B" commercial pilot's license by the time she was twenty. She was only the third woman in England to attain this rating.

With money gathered from these recitals and aviation articles written for magaziens, she bought a two-seater Spartan airplane on the installment plan, and started a small business called Air Trips, Ltd. Her partner in this enterprise was Dorothy Spicer, whom she had met when they were both taking a course in engineering at the London Aeroplane Club. It was Dorothy's job to act as ground engineer and be entirely responsible for the maintenance of all equipment, while Pauline gave joy-rides to any who would fly with her, and taxied passengers from one field to another.

Some of the local people had little inclination to go

up in a plane piloted by a woman. Pauline had a mongrel terrier named Wendy who went everywhere with her, and was always very much in evidence at any field where she stopped to give rides. One time Pauline asked a group of people standing near if they would like to take flight tickets. One man looked at her aghast: "Wot, us fly! No perishing fear! Why even the blinkin dog's called 'Windy.' "

In spite of a certain amount of public reluctance, quite common in those days, the Gower-Spicer business enterprise flourished for seven years, interspersed from time to time by air carnivals. One summer the two girls visited 185 towns on one of these air-circus tours, doing aerial acrobatics for an excited audience and giving rides to any who were interested in getting a taste of flying for themselves. All of this gave Pauline fine experience for the work she was to do later, when war came to England. By 1936 she had piloted more than 33,000 passengers.

She continued to do aviation writing too. In 1934 she wrote a collection of short poems with the interesting title: *Piffling Poems for Pilots,* and in 1937 her book, with typical simplicity called *Women with Wings,* appeared. In it she predicted that should war come, there would be a great need for women pilots. Two years later her prophecy came true. Only war emergency such as England faced in her darkest hour during the first two years of the conflict would have persuaded a conservative British Air Ministry to use women pilots to ferry planes. Tremendous reserves of air power were needed to protect England's shores from invasion.

In this same book, Pauline advised women pilots in

the United States to get properly organized for service while that country was still at peace. She felt that then was the time to do it, for there would be a great need for all kinds of ferry and communications work in a country with such vast distances as the United States. One has only to think back to the desperate pilot shortage in this country in the days when the Women's Auxiliary Ferrying Squadron was formed to realize that Pauline Gower knew what she was talking about.

The busiest people usually can find time to do just a few more things, so Pauline found time during these crowded years to become district commissioner of the Girl Guides in Kent, an organization in which she took a very active interest before the war. Now that the European war is over, she has renewed her close alliance with it.

For her fine work as president of the Gillingham Corps of the St. John's Ambulance Brigade in the days just prior to the war, she was awarded the order of St. John of Jerusalem.

In 1937 Pauline made her first real entry into another phase of aviation, which was to become her deepest interest as soon as the war emergency had ended. She became a member of the Gorell Committee, set up by the air minister to promote civil aviation. As a logical result of her fine work on this committee, she was appointed to the board of the British Overseas Airways Corporation. This national organization for civilian flying interests in Britain is comparable to the Civil Aeronautics Authority in the United States. Since the European war ended, this has been her chief aviation activity. Not long ago she made a survey of routes through Africa and the Middle East for the B.O.A.C.

But from 1939 to 1945 her work with the A.T.A. brought all Pauline's other activities to a temporary halt. She was soon given complete charge of the difficult problem of allocating machines so that each pilot could do her most efficient ferrying with the least amount of overlapping. Because of the ever increasing pressure of administrative duties, by the second year of the war Pauline was forced to give up most of the actual flying duties and leave them to other members of the group. By this time girls had been recruited from France, America, New Zealand, South Africa, Canada, and even one top-notch woman pilot from Chile who had to take lessons in English before she could take the basic flight course.

As many as seven hundred applications a day came from all corners of the earth for admission to the Women's Division of the A.T.A., but Pauline Gower maintained such high standards that even at the end of the war, there were only little more than one hundred women in the group.

As Commander Gower put it: "These girls were the cream of the flying crop—physically perfect and mentally satisfied, whatever their other differences!"

They came from all walks of life and are returning to them now that the war is over. The youngest was twenty, the oldest a grandmother, with a son in the U.S. Air Corps. All had good eyesight and good judgment primarily, and confidence without being overconfident. Only women with wide and varied flying experience were chosen.

"A ferry pilot had to be highly adaptable," Commander Gower insisted; "the work demanded it. They had to fly as many as five different aircraft in a single day sometimes. I have found that women are either very good pilots or very bad ones, they don't seem to run to mediocrity. Men are different, they can stooge along in comfortable mediocrity for months, then suddenly find themselves, but that doesn't seem to happen to women in my experience. We could tell very quickly into which class our applicants fell, and although I hate to generalize on any qualities of difference between men and women pilots, I think I may safely say that women are more cautious than men. This is no yellow streak—but they are less likely to take foolish chances. They feel that it's better to be *a* late pilot, than *the* late pilot!"

One of the American girls in the group summed it up nicely when she said: "It was two strikes out of three against women pilots in the beginning anyway, so we were extra conscientious and very determined not to have anyone say—'just another woman pilot!' "

In the beginning the authorities had said: "The hand that rocks the cradle wrecks the crate"—jokingly, of course, but they gave them only the older planes to fly, nevertheless. It didn't take the girls long to prove that such misgivings were needless, for between January, 1939, and April, 1941, they delivered 1,600 planes with only four accidents. Two were due very obviously to aircraft faults, and one was an unexplained crash in which a woman student was flying with a man instructor.

It was no uncommon experience for one of the girls to fly four different ships, covering 2,000 miles and visiting each county of the British Isles, in a single day. And throughout the five years of their service, their safety record was very much better than the Men's Division of the A.T.A.

The girls were particularly pleased with the way the men in the A.T.A. accepted them as colleagues in a short time and worked with them on an equal footing. As one London girl said: "There was no tea-party atmosphere about that show!"

They were always busy and happy—proud to use their skill in Britain's war effort. They worked hard, reporting at eight in the morning and flying until sundown. Sometimes they were not finished even then, for if a girl had delivered a plane to a distant airfield, she often had to spend the night in a tedious train journey back to headquarters.

Ferry pilots did not fly at night because of the danger of enemy aircraft overhead. The war was very near and enemy aircraft was always a possible hazard, even in the day time, though seldom realized. The ships flown by the A.T.A. were unarmed and the only possible action while flying was to watch carefully for enemy ships and get out of the way quickly if any appeared. They knew that German raiders would not hesitate to shoot down a defenseless plane and that they would have little chance to get away, but they took these risks casually. Flying in a group, they formed a line astern (the opposite of a V formaiton), the international formation for noncombatant aircraft. Then they kept a sharp lookout for enemy raiders.

One day two of the girls were pilot and copilot of a twin-engined bomber being flown to a base in southern England, when a German swooped down out of a cloud, taking a few pot shots at their ship as he passed.

They were plenty scared, but he didn't turn for a second attack, and no one was hurt.

Four very real hazards were always present, however. The weather was a constant enemy, as they had no radios and on long trips were entirely dependent on meteorological knowledge they had picked up before starting. No sudden changes in weather could be radioed to them.

"England is noted for its foul and ridiculously unstable weather," one of the group said, "so I wasn't surprised on one trip in a Spitfire to find that, after having left the airdrome in bright sunshine, I was forced down ten minutes later to within fifty feet of the ground by clouds and low visibility."

But the A.T.A.—"Ancient and Tattered Airmen" and "Always Terrified Airwomen," as the A.T.A. men and women pilots laughingly called themselves, just took it in their stride. They prided themselves on getting planes through in bad weather, knowing that any delay, however small, hindered the war effort.

Then, of course, there was pilot error, the human factor, when a tired pilot makes mistakes she would not ordinarily make. The girls were closely watched for signs of strain and fatigue.

"This was not special consideration though," Miss Gower hastened to add; "the men were watched just as carefully. Don't misunderstand me, either, I'm not saying that men and women pilots are exactly alike. They certainly are not. It mattered tremendously to a tense, nervous woman when she was sent as a stranger into a rough station, while a man probably didn't mind it in the least. This was one reason why I liked to choose the personnel myself and tried to know the temperament of each pilot. That was important if they were to do their best work. But I made it my business to see that each airdrome commander was unaware specifically that there were women there; for him there were just pilots."

The unservicability of aircraft was a third hazard, a very serious one in the early days of the war when planes were being rushed off the assembly line at factories, so greatly needed that there was barely time to check their airworthiness. Later, of course, as the tide of the European battle turned, these planes were more uniformly tested before being ferried to air bases.

The navigation hazard was probably the worst of all —barrage balloons, artillery ranges, and R.A.F. training schools had to be dodged. Ferry pilots in the United States never had these difficulties, any more than ferry pilots in England had long navigation distances to worry about. Each pilot flying over the British Isles had to plot her course very carefully at the base. The destination was never marked on a map, the pilot had to memorize it and the route to be flown. It was a trying job, for there was no such thing as the shortest distance between two points, no straight lines. Wide detours had to be made to avoid balloon barrages and convoy routes protected by "ack-ack." Even the shortest trip had to be made in a series of zig-zag hops, and when the pilot arrived at the base she had to take certain steps to be recognized as friendly before being allowed to land.

Even after her pilots had delivered their valuable cargoes, Pauline Gower's job was only half done. She had to see to it that they were brought back to the home base before night, otherwise there would not be enough pilots available for the following day's work. There must have been many times when she wished she were just another ferry pilot with the rest of the group.

Pauline still insisted: "I was just a taxi pilot before the war, there is nothing special about me. I just happened to have a little administrative ability and a background of experience in aviation, so they gave me the job."

She forgot to mention, of course, that she was the third woman in England to hold a "B" commercial license, for which she had to pass advanced tests in night and blind flying, navigation, and meteorology. She also holds a radio operator's license and first-class navigator's license—all of which makes her without a doubt the most highly qualified woman flyer in England. It took considerable digging to uncover that she also had been made a member of the Order of the British Empire in 1942 and a Fellow of the Royal Meteorological Society, to say nothing of being made vice-president of the Federation of British Professional Women, and council member of the Women's Engineering Society. She doesn't think there is anything very special about her, but the world of aviation and all who know her personally disagree.

Today the future of the British Overseas Airways Corporation is her direct concern. Not long ago she made a speech at a meeting of high government officials in aviation in which she outlined the role she thought the organization should play in the postwar world, in a sound and definite way. Sir Robert Gower, in the audience, received many congratulations on the fine speech his daughter had made.

When the British fighting forces needed every man

who could handle the controls of a bomber or pursuit plane, much of the flying behind the lines was done by this modest battalion of bird-women. They worked day and night ferrying planes from the end of the assembly line to men waiting to take them across the channel to invasion bases. Behind them worked other women, flight engineers, operation officers, and aircraft mechanics. But in spite of all this, the postwar picture for British women in commercial aviation is none too bright.

"I don't hold out any rosy prospect for women commercial pilots or engineers in this country now that the war is over," Pauline Gower says, "There are thousands of trained R.A.F. men wanting aviation jobs now that peace has come again to the world, and personally I doubt that women will have much of a chance in commercial aviation, as pilots or engineers. Before the war, women were not in the field of commercial transportation; there were no women engineers on trains, engineers or navigators on ships, or public transport bus drivers. It is no more likely that they will be taken on as airline pilots, though of course they may be employed in a few smaller aircraft companies as ferry pilots and taxi pilots."

She hastened to add that, of course, this was only her personal opinion and that she might be wrong but that she thought it a pity to encourage the hopes of young girls and let them embark on plans for a career in commercial aviation in England when their aspirations have so little chance of being realized.

"As one final word, I should like to say," she concludes, "that this lack of opportunity in flying jobs for women is no reflection on the ability of women pilots.

Anyone who knows in this country is more than ready to admit after the fine work of the women in the A.T.A. during the war that the individual woman pilot is just as good as the individual man pilot, but economics and peacetime philosophy will change the employment picture just the same. Women will still find their best peacetime aviation jobs as air hostesses and other nonpilot positions."

LOIS COOTS TONKIN

AVIATION's greatest enemy today is the weather. There is no other factor in flying over which we have so little control—and need so much. The meteorologist, whose duty it is to predict the weather through which all pilots must fly, knows that it will never be wholly conquered. Through scientific knowledge and experience, however, we have learned to utilize the weather instead of fighting it.

The meteorologist is no weather maker, but he knows in advance what conditions will be because he has learned through hard work and study to be wise in the ways of wind and temperature, humidity and barometric pressure. The weather forecaster can accurately gage changes in these elements in advance. On the strength of the meteorologist's advice, air lines operate or remain idle, and at his unofficial command, military planes are grounded.

Today man can fly, when formerly he would have been earthbound, because of his greater knowledge of the atmosphere, his conquest of the air. Mark Twain's comment that "everyone talks about the weather but no one does anything about it" is no longer true—the modern meteorologist does plenty!

As the war clouds descended, the government

weather bureaus began to suffer from the draft of man-
power the same as hundreds of other agencies, and one
more job previously thought to be strictly within man's
prerogative was opened to women. For the first time in
its seventy-year history, the Weather Bureau in 1940
began training girls for the varied and responsible job
of meteorologist.

Five universities in the country (Massachusetts Institute of Technology, New York University, California Institute of Technology, University of Chicago,
and University of California at Los Angeles) offered
graduate scholarships for a year's work in meteorology.
At first these opportunities were offered only to men
with four years of college (including a year of calculus
and a year of physics) and a private pilot's license, but
by March, 1942, the scholarships were open to women
who could meet the same requirements.

The girls were told that, if they completed this eight
months' course successfully, they would be employed
at Washington or at one of the outlying government
stations with a professional rating of junior meteorologist. The starting salary would be $2,000 plus over-
time, and the job would include weather observing and
forecasting, research, training of personnel, and miscellaneous work connected with the running of a weather-
bureau station.

Very few women in the country could meet these
high requirements. In fact even today, six years after
the first scholarship was offered, there are only eight
women professional meteorologists in the whole country. But as the need for meteorologists grew, standards
were lowered and high-school graduates were trained
to help prepare weather maps, on a subprofessional

level as weather observers. These girls hold the majority of meteorological jobs today.

Lois Coots, one of the eight professional women
meteorologists in the United States, was probably the
first to be granted a meteorology scholarship by the
Civil Aeronautics Authority. At Marietta College in
Ohio this intelligent West Virginia girl had been
studying pre-med for four years and was all set to
enter medical school and become a doctor. Then one
day a friend dared her to go up in his airplane with
him. With that very first flight, her medical ambitions
became a thing of the past—the fascination of flying
had a grip on her.

Luck was with her! The next year she was admitted
to Marietta's Civilian Pilot Training Program and was
soon on the way to a pilot's license.

"It was my instructor, Lenore Harper McElroy, who
made me want to be a part of aviation mare than anything. She was a 'natural' pilot, the No. 1 woman flyer
of Indiana. She and her husband were assigned to instruct our C.P.T. group—twenty-eight boys and two
girls. Each instructor had fourteen boys and one girl.

"Because I was her first girl student, Lenore saw to
it that I got all the breaks! She soloed me first and
helped me be the first of the group to get a license.
One of the boys, Roger Dyar, who later broke the
world's speed record when he dived his P-47 at 627
miles an hour, was a very clever cartoonist and he covered the bulletin board in 'the ready room' with a sequence of drawings aimed at the injustice of it all.

"One showed a line of boys clear around the airport
waiting for Lenore to fly with them, with my slacks

clearly recognizable at the very end of the line. Lenore is saying: 'I believe it's your turn, Lois.'

"Another, I remember, showed me coming in for a landing, bouncing about fifteen feet into the air after my wheels touch. Lenore on the ground has her face turned away and is saying to the inspector: 'She always makes a perfect spot landing right on the circle.' We really had a lot of fun!"

When Lois' group had completed the C.P.T. course, Lenore was offered a flight instructor's position at Hartung Field in Detroit and persuaded Lois to go along as a ground-school instructor. There Lois taught meteorology, civil air regulations and navigation.

When the C.A.A. weather bureau, its staff dwindled to something less than a skeleton because of the draft, decided with quaking hearts to grant a few scholarships to women for meteorological training, Lois' professor of physics at Marietta called her long distance to see if she would be inetrested. She was, and luckily could meet all the requirements. Soon Lois found herself the only girl in a class of two hundred navy ensigns, army cadets, and C.A.A. weather-bureau personnel, studying meteorology at New York University.

Eight months later she was the first woman meteorologist at the government weather bureau in Washington, plotting maps and charts, decoding teletype reports, checking dew point, pressure areas, and cloud formations—all that goes into the preparation of an individual weather report every six hours.

Many more meteorologists were needed, so the C.A.A. sent Lois on a six weeks' recruiting tour all over the midwestern states to interest other girls in taking the meteorology course. She spent most of her time speaking at women's colleges, some as far west as Kansas. It certainly wasn't Lois' fault that the trip wasn't more of a success!

"Women usually consider calculus and physics rather dry and colorless subjects and shy away from them in college," she said upon her return to Washington, "so I found very few with such training plus a private pilot's license."

Back in Washington, Lois became assistant chief of the Training Division, answering a great many questions about training programs which came in from women all over the country. Another part of her work was with the Civil Service Commission, making out various tests for prospective meteorologists and keeping a close check on the progress of students after they had been selected.

That was not all Lois did in Washington however! She took time out to marry Lieut. Henry Tonkin, and she transferred to Detroit airport to be near her husband until he went overseas. In December of 1944 they became the proud parents of a baby son who, they both aver, will one day be "the best darn flyer and weatherman in the world." Which would make it a flying and weather-conscious family—Lieutenant Tonkin of the Navy is—you guessed it—a meteorologist and pilot! During the war he was in England, forecasting weather for channel operations.

In Detroit Lois did much more advanced work in actual forecasting. "My job in Detroit was quite different from the one in Washington. It was the type of work for which I had been trained at New York University. I worked in shifts along with several other meteorologists. There were four maps a day to be drawn and analyzed which meant there must always be at least one professional meteorologist on duty to do the analysis and give the forecast. We all helped with the observations, which were taken every half hour.

"It was a very busy and interesting job. Pilots were always in the office, getting the latest weather along their routes. It had its amusing aspects too, because the public was continually calling up to ask if the day would be all right to hang out clothes, or if a picnic could be planned for Sunday. One day a woman even called me to ask if I would advise putting a sweater on her six-months-old baby when she took it out."

If you had walked into Lois' office in Detroit, a rather strange picture would have been laid out before you. The first thing to greet your eyes, and your ears, even before the slim, dark-haired girl stepped forward to welcome you, would be the three teletype machines, ticking away like the machines in a stock-exchange room. Pertinent weather information from every part of the country is relayed into the Detroit station. Thousands of stations all over the United States, in an intricate network of observation posts, send in data on the weather in their particular sections.

To other stations all over the country the home station at Detroit also sends out its messages at prearranged intervals in this order: station, ceiling, sky condition, visibility, present weather, obstructions to vision, barometric pressure, temperature, dew point, wind direction and velocity, altimeter setting, and any pertinent remarks. All this comes through the paper in symbols which are meaningless to the average person—they represent the shorthand of the weather-man.

Through the office window, outside in a well-ventilated shelter, you would see an intricate-looking thermograph. This is an automatic temperature recorder—a cylinder revolving with clock-like precision while an inked needle traces an indelible path along the graph covering the cylinder. This graph is calibrated in degrees of temperature Fahrenheit; so that, by consulting the recording, the weatherman knows the given temperature for any minute of the day or night, and the graph stands as a permanent record for reference. This is how a newspaper report accurately checks the hottest day for the date in ten years or the coldest day on record.

Inside the office a long mahogany panel attached vertically to the wall holds a glass tube filled with mercury. This is not a thermometer but a standard mercury barometer denoting barometric pressure in inches of mercury. Investigation shows that at the moment we are in the center of a low-pressure area—with the barometer falling rapidly. Therefore a storm of considerable intensity is expected within a few hours.

On another wall are two large dials—twin faces grinning at the mad rush that is taking place in the office. One face records wind direction and is divided into compass headings of north, south, east, and west, and all the intermediate segments of 360 degrees. Today the wind is from due east. The second face is calibrated for m.p.h. velocity of the wind—it registers twenty-eight now but fresh gusts make it spurt up to thirty-two at times.

Above Lois' desk is a chart which acts as a guide in

determining the visibility at the moment. It reads: town hall—one mile, petroleum tank—two miles, Wheatley Hills—three miles. She looks out of the window toward these objects; and, by noting the most distant one that she can see, she determines visibility.

From time to time Lois goes outside and releases a helium-filled weather balloon. As it floats upward, she takes periodic readings through an instrument resembling a combination sextant and telescope, called a theodolite. With it she can determine the accurate ceiling and the wind velocity and direction at various altitudes. This is very important for the pilots of airliners and other big ships who want to fly at the altitude giving them the most favorable winds.

Some weather stations also send up a radiosonde. This is similar to the helium-filled balloon but has a miniature high-frequency radio set attached to it. As the balloon floats upward, the radio transmits a record of the temperature, humidity, and atmospheric pressure at different altitudes to the observer on the ground. At seventy thousand feet the balloon bursts, a small parachute opens, and the radio set floats safely down to earth.

Meteorology is not yet an exact science, but much progress has been made toward that goal. Weather trends can now be predicted with a high percentage of accuracy for as long as two weeks in advance. Actual weather conditions can be forecast accurately for twenty-four to thirty-six hours ahead.

Lois explained how this has come about: "With the development of the air-mass analysis method by the Norwegian school of meteorologists, the science of weather forecasting began to come into its own. They advanced the theory that weather was caused by the interaction between huge masses of air having different geographical sources and therefore different physical properties.

"The boundaries between these air masses from different sources they called 'fronts'—'cold front' if a cold air mass is displacing a warm one, and 'warm front' in the reverse case. With this workable theory as a basis, plus a network of observation stations and some knowledge of the upper air, meteorologists were soon able to work out accurate methods of weather forecasting.

"Three different methods were developed, each independent enough of the other to be used as a check. In the 'front method' the past displacements of air masses and fronts are noted and a new displacement computed in line with former ones. The 'geostrophic wind method' computes this displacement from the winds aloft. The 'tendency method' uses the barometric tendency as the basis for computing the new movement. The experienced forecaster makes three checks on himself therefore; and, after adding modifications according to the air-mass analysis theory, he is able to issue a forecast that is as accurate as science has been able to discover to date.

"This is no crystal-ball art—it is a scientific, mathematically sound deduction. Long-range forecasts predicting weather trends for several weeks ahead are based on the fact that weather runs in cycles, and similar symptoms are likely to produce similar results. With the further development of radio and radar equipment, we are well on the way to victory over the elements."

Before long Weather Bureau officials were issuing

public statements of their satisfaction with the work the girls were doing. Chief Meteorologist R. E. Spencer said: "Our women meteorologists compare very favorably with the men of equal training and experience. They can do some of the work better because they are neater and possess such a sense of responsibility."

The weather over every mile of a pilot's flight is checked by the meteorologist, who gives the pilot information that often spells the difference between safety and danger when areas of icing conditions, thunder storms, violent winds, poor visibility, or low ceilings lie in his flight path. Obviously this is a great responsibility and a meteorologist must be alert, have sound judgment, and above all have the ability to visualize conditions which he can't actually see. Lois, in her daily work, must deal with masses of air that blanket half a dozen states, bounded by "fronts" thousands of miles long. She must see these things in her imagination and interpret them in terms of weather conditions for distant areas as well as for her particular community.

If you're the first in any field, you meet with a certain amount of prejudice as well as distinction, but as Lois says: "Once the initial prejudice against women ran its course, nary a complaint was heard from any of our male associates. As a matter of fact, they were soon asking for more women to do the same type of work."

As a nation at war, we learned that weather may be a valuable ally or a deadly foe. A battle can be lost or won because of weather. We all know that aircraft may be saved from destruction because the meteorologist warns against ice or fog, but few of us realize how wide-spread the importance of weather knowledge is over all branches of the armed forces. Weather is a valuable weapon if you know how to use it.

At first it helped Germany and Japan in their aggression. The advance knowledge that September, 1939, would bring clear skies in Poland for his bombers and firm ground for his ground forces strengthened Hitler's blows. But how well Germany remembers its winter-defeated armies in Russia!

The Jap sneak attack on Pearl Harbor was a weather success too. Before the actual attack, Jap aircraft carriers loaded with planes ready for the zero hour sneaked hundreds of miles eastward under the cover of large storm clouds. After Pearl Harbor we turned the tables. Before our attack on Guadalcanal, the stage was set for successful operations by a forecast of many days of foggy clouds. This screened our advance naval units from Jap air attack. Followed by the clear, bright sunshine which experts had predicted, the weather cooperated nicely for beach landings.

Before the war, collection of weather data was carried out cooperatively on an international scale. Periodically at the same Greenwich-meridian time, observers at land stations throughout the world turned toward the sky and took readings from their recording instruments. Observers on ships lowered buckets into the sea to find out the temperature there. All this assorted information was radioed to collection centers. Then by radio and teletype the more important facts went to forecasters in all parts of the world. They, in turn, plotted, analyzed, and distributed weather information to pilots, railroad men, newspapers, farmers, utility companies—one could compile an enormous list of persons who depend on the meteorologist for help in their work.

Outbreak of war brought this set-up to a temporary halt. Censorship labeled all weather data confidential and weather forecasts, except for sketchy local ones, no longer appeared in the press. And then gradually, as the war favorably progressed and the fear of invasion subsided, the meteorologists' skill was once more available to everyone.

The future possibilities for women in meteorology are unlimited. It is a field in which women have proved that they can do as well as or better than men. The Weather Bureau will undoubtedly continue to employ women on both the subprofessional and professional levels. Air lines and private concerns will also offer jobs to the trained meteorologist.

There are hundreds of subprofessional observers extremely interested in the work, who are doing a really fine job. They work in shifts and are out in all kinds of weather to take the observations, but it doesn't seem to bother them a bit.

Probably the most important job done by these weather observers is the plotting of maps. They work with printed maps of the United States on which names of towns and cities are indicated by code, to avoid the confusion of having all names written out. The girls interpret the symbols coming in over the teletype and transfer them to the maps. All points of the same atmospheric pressure are connected, arrows show wind direction, and an "S" and "R" indicate places where there is snow or rain. These maps give a complete picture of the weather, even indicating the direction in which "fronts" are moving.

"I would say that a few of the qualities which make for success in this field are dependability, genuine interest in weather and its scientific background, the ability to get along with people of all types, and a real interest in a continually expanding subject," Lois adds. "I see no reason why women should not advance as rapidly as men in the field."

Meteorology offers a splendid future for young people. It has a special appeal to their pioneering spirit because it too is young and has far to go.

NANCY LOVE

"CINCINNATI, OHIO, June 26, 1943 (A.P.).—A B-25 Mitchell bomber, racing hundreds of miles in record time from the west, circled a midwestern airport, nosed into the wind and landed today, writing another chapter in the history of women in aviation, according to an announcement made by the Army Air Corps Ferrying Division Headquarters. This was the first time in American military history that a woman pilot and copilot delivered a bombing plane on part of its trip from factory to front line. The pilot was Nancy Love of Boston, Senior Squadron Commander of the newly formed Women's Auxiliary Ferrying Squadron, and the copilot, Barbara Towne of California, another member of the W.A.F.S."

For Nancy Love, appointed to her post by the Secretary of War less than a year after Pearl Harbor, this trip was the realization of a dream. Here was undisputable proof of her belief that women pilots could relieve men pilots for actual combat duty by ferrying ships from factory to field.

The formation of the W.A.F.S. fulfilled the dream of every American girl flyer—the twenty-five girls in this original group, the hundreds later given flight training in Texas for the ferry command, the thousands whose flight paths have been established today and tomorrow.

Nancy Love, at twenty-eight, brought to her duties as chief of the first American group of women ferry pilots a variety of experiences you would normally expect to find only in a woman half again her age. This slim, gracious, blue-eyed young lady, with attractive gray hair framing a youthful face, was then a veteran pilot of twelve years' experience.

"Nancy was the ideal choice for squadron commander," one WAF said, "because above all else she is a top-notch pilot with a tremendous enthusiasm for flying."

Anyone who has ever flown with Nancy Love can tell you what a resourceful pilot she is. An army officer who checked her out on a B-17 tells this story about "one of the coolest and best students" he ever had.

"We had piled up fifty hours in ten days on this B-17, day and night and instrument flying. On the last landing just before we began the final approach, I cut the switches of three of the four engines without any warning, by way of a practice forced landing. I wasn't feeling too easy myself as I did it—one motor isn't much to have left on that ship. Nancy never turned a hair. Without the slightest change in expression she brought us in for a perfect landing."

A few months after the United States entered the war, a soft-spoken young woman was thoughtfully discussing with army "brass hats" the possibility of a women's ferry pilot group in the United States similar to Pauline Gower's A.T.A. group in Britain. Her ideas were sound and practical, and her presentation eloquent. The general was thoroughly convinced.

"Women pilots will first be used to deliver to the

army the multitude of small training planes now pouring off the assembly lines of the aircraft companies," he
announced. "We want to tap the reservoir of experienced women pilots which we know to exist. And if
they show in time that they can fly four-motored bombers safely after a proper period of training and prelim-
inary work, I see no reason why they may not do so."

So the experiment was launched, Nancy very confident that it would be a success.

Nancy certainly never imagined herself a bomber pilot back in 1930, when she was first introduced to airplanes. At an age when most girls were learning "The
Black Bottom," sixteen-year-old Nancy Harkness was
learning to fly. That summer a pair of barnstormers
flew into her home town in Michigan, offering flights
in a Fleet and Stinson to whoever would go up with
them. Nancy spent most of her spare time watching
them and taking occasional hops whenever she could
dig up the price of a ride. Before the summer ended
she'd made up her mind that she wanted to learn to fly
herself.

Her family, like so many others, did not share her
enthusiasm for the idea, but they weakened under Nancy's persuasion. Arrangements were made with the
owner of the Fleet for instruction.

A race against time was soon in full swing. Nancy
had to leave for school in Massachusetts in two weeks
and she wanted to make a first solo before she left. Another race soon paralleled the first because one of
Nancy's friends decided he would learn to fly at the
same time, and the two had a friendly competition to
see who would make the first solo flight.

A sleepy instructor was frequently aroused before

daylight by one or the other trying to get a head start on the day's flying, but he was game, even when Nancy pulled him out one morning at four to crowd in the last few hours. In less than two weeks she soloed and secured the few hours then necessary for a private "ticket." She also won in the race with her friend—by a hair—Nancy soloing in the morning, the other student in the afternoon of the same day.

Then off to Milton Academy she went for her last year. The school authorities were not very air-minded and students were forbidden to fly. Nancy and her brother did a little flying at a Boston airport, and no one would have been the wiser if the two hadn't yielded to temptation and "buzzed" the school just once too often, in wall-shaking proximity. Milton's head mistress was able to identify the plane and trace the occupants, and Nancy was offered an alternative between suspension and giving up her flying activities. To all appearances she did give up flying then; but, by elaborate arrangement with two commercial operators on Cape Cod, she still managed to get in some flying time week ends.

In the fall of 1931 Nancy entered Vassar. She completely gave up flying for one semester at her parents' request and consequently received good grades, but as her interest in flying reasserted itself, her grades dropped. By June she had a limited commercial license to show for her flying activities, but was on scholastic probation for her classroom accomplishments.

She climaxed the school year by spinning in as a passenger in a Great Lakes training plane. The pilot was badly hurt but Nancy apparently uninjured. A month later, when Nancy spoke to her physician father about not feeling up to par, he made an examination and found she had fractured her skull in the crack-up.

The next fall Nancy again returned to Vassar with a commercial license in her hand, but this time left at Christmas because of ill health. It seemed as if she just wasn't destined for a college education! By this time aviation was so much a part of her life that she decided to begin a flying career in earnest. Intelligently realizing that a college degree is not an end in itself, and that she was better fitted for other things, she said good-by to Vassar without regret.

Today Nancy laughs at her naive attempts to break into aviation in the midst of a depression which had even experienced men pilots looking for work. Needless to say, she didn't find a flying job waiting for her.

Her parents were still not very much in sympathy with her flying ambitions anyway, so they offered to send Nancy to New York for a secretarial course. She went, since there was nothing else to be done at the moment, and dabbled lightly in shorthand and typing. Most of her time, however, and the greater part of her spending money were used to shoot across the river to Newark and pile up as many hours in the air as possible.

Through one of the casual contacts you sometimes make which change your whole life, Nancy landed a flying job the next spring selling airplanes and flight instruction for a newly formed company in Boston. The job didn't involve too much actual flying at first, but at least it brought her into close association with airplanes and pilots—one pilot in particular—a tall, blond go-getter who had started the company. Bob Love's enthusiasm for aviation while he was a student at Massachusetts Institute of Technology had made him, like Nancy, forego a degree. He left college to develop an aviation center in Boston. There he had established his career by being practically a one-man airport—chartering planes, giving instruction, promoting airplane sales, and even keeping the company records.

Nancy had a lot of fun trying to sell aviation to the New England public. A few did buy airplanes and courses of instruction, but more important to Nancy was the valuable experience she gained, flying many different ships.

In September, 1935, Nancy joined the Bureau of Air Commerce in its air-making project, taking in the east-coast area and covering every city in New York State. With two other women, Nancy embarked on this government program to mark 16,000 cities and towns for the benefit of flyers. Their job was to locate suitable spots for air markers and persuade owners to put these marks on their roofs or other suitable places. The idea was to make the air lanes safe and surer for transport planes and their passengers and to help the private flyer going cross country on his own.

They marked the country off in fifteen-mile squares and tried to get at least one marker at every intersection of these lines. When the war came, all this work had to be undone because in case of invasion such markers would guide the enemy. Now that the war is over, a larger program of air-marking is again under way.

Before Nancy had been with the bureau a year, she and Bob announced their engagement and she quit her job to take a wedding trip to the west coast in a Beechcraft.

A few months later they decided to fly to Los Angeles for the National Air Races. Just before they left, Nancy found that the the Beechcraft Company had entered her name in the Amelia Earhart trophy race. She wasn't a bit pleased at the prospect because she had had absolutely no experience with pylon flying. She didn't want to be called "scary" though, so she decided to see it through.

That race was a nightmare. Nancy overshot all her turns badly and grew angrier with every pylon she rounded. It was a sorely ruffled young lady who came down the home stretch, the more so because Bob had seemed more concerned about his landing gear than his wife's neck. He had told her at least a hundred times not to forget to lower the wheels. With an "I'll show him" she climbed up to 2,000 feet and deliberately lowered and raised the wheels several times in front of the thousands of spectators for Bob's benefit, then landed.

Even after Nancy got back to Boston she was still mad about the whole experience, so she arranged with Monocoupe for a plane to enter the Detroit races. She finished the pylon race in second place this time and returned to Boston feeling much better, but definitely through with that type of flying for all time.

Nancy was about to continue her air-marking work when she was asked to demonstrate and test experimental airplane designs for the Gwinn Aircar Company. She was very much interested in this revolutionary model with its tricycle landing gear, so she readily agreed to test it for Joe Gwinn.

One morning, at dawn to get the quietest air, a specially designed airplane that besides its tricycle landing gear also had only a single-control column (a joy stick with a steering wheel on it) which eliminated rudder pedals, was seen at Consolidated Field in Buffalo coming down from high altitude in elevator-like landings, hitting the ground with terrific force. In the right-hand seat sat Joe Gwinn, nonchalantly working a slide rule and making mental calculations, quite unconcerned about the violent maneuvers the airplane under him was making.

There were no dual controls, so Nancy in the pilot's seat was doing all the flying.

As the tests progressed, every flying instinct Nancy had was violated as Joe insisted that the plane be brought down from two thousand feet like a rock and strike the ground with the stick full back, flaps down, and engine throttled so that it landed with full force on the landing gear. The first time they tried it she gave in to the pilot's natural instinct and relaxed on the stick just before they touched the ground, spoiling the test.

Joe looked reproachful. "Now Nancy, that won't do, this plane is designed to withstand certain strain—and we must find out if it will do it. We must see how much punishment the undercarriage will take without breaking."

In the weird half light of the next morning they tried it again. The plane shot down from two thousand feet at close to a thousand feet a minute in a straight perpendicular drop. "Those last two thousand feet were the worst experience I've ever had in my life," Nancy said later; "the ground rushed up at us with unbelievable speed. My insides felt sort of shriveled up and I know I was holding my breath as we dropped like a plummet onto the runway. I could tell the impact was tremendous from the explosive sounds of the oleo shock absorbers, but though I had expected to be bodily pushed through the seat, I felt only a slight jar."

Joe was extremely gratified. His faith has been justified, his calculations worked out. Nancy hoped that one such effort would satisfy him, but no, she had to repeat it—again and again. Joe inspecting the landing gear carefully after each test. A completely exhausted Nancy staggered home at the end of the day, and at the end of every day for two weeks.

When the landing gear cracked one day on a perfectly normal landing, in one of those freak accidents you can never believe unless you're there to see it, Nancy's only comment was:

"Heaven help us if the landing gear had given way on one of the violent tests!"

Joe had the landing gear fixed and the tests went on.

Nancy remained with Gwinn for a year after that, doing routine testing and demonstrating. Although she hadn't been too sure at first about Joe's creation, she was completely won over by its performance in these tests. She shared Joe's enthusiasm and became an enthusiastic champion of the features incorporated in the Aircar. Anything that promoted safety in flying always received her wholehearted support, for that was Nancy's chief interest—to sell the airplane as a safe and pleasant means of travel to the American public. Such ideas were temporarily shelved for the war, but they were too deep seated ever to be given up.

In June, 1940, France sent out an SOS for planes of all types to be used for patrol purposes, and Nancy had her first experience ferrying military aircraft. The planes were flown to a point on the Canadian border, dragged across the line by hand in accordance with U.S. neutrality regulations. The pilots then resumed their mass delivery flight to the point of embarkation.

The climax of a brilliant career in aviation for Nancy Love was the formation of the W.A.F.S. with Nancy as executive officer. From hundreds of women who applied, a picked group of twenty-five was chosen. One had been an instructor at Pearl Harbor on December 7, another a test pilot for a private aircraft corporation. For some it was their first experience at professional flying, their flying activities having been previously limited to Sunday hops at the local airport. But whatever their backgrounds, all were competent pilots.

Each applicant had to have at least 500 hours certified time in her logbook (though it turned out that the average time in the air of the original twenty-five was 1162 hours apiece), a 200-horsepower rating, and perfect physical condition. They looked very capable in their smart gray twill suits, built more for utility than beauty.

Headquarters were set up in Wilmington, Delawere, and the girls given a course in army procedure. They started flying primary trainers; but, as their experience and fine record proved them capable, they went on to bigger ships. Twenty-nine hundred army planes were safely ferried by this small group in ten months' time. Before the group was disbanded they were flying four-motored bombers, even a few B-29 Superfortresses. In the last few months of its existance, a greatly expanded group was flying the equivalent of six times around the earth every day.

Nancy always bent over backward obeying army

rules, and was reluctant to talk about herself when reporters inevitably asked for interviews.

"I'm not much at making statements," she'd say; "I'm just plain Mrs. Love trying to do well the job I have to do, which is ferrying airplanes within the continental United States. Don't present us as a glamour outfit, we're not. There's no room or time for glamour in the W.A.F.S., we've got a serious job to do. If any of these girls came here with illusions, things like icy winds, murky skies, and long hours in the air in open cockpits will take it out of them quickly enough."

The W.A.F.S. were soon operating on regular schedules, through heat and cold. Their work was sometimes hazardous, and a great responsibility rested on each WAF's soulders, for she was in full charge of the airplane from the moment she climbed into the cockpit until a receipt was given at the end of the trip for the plane's safe delivery.

Each trip had to be "flown on paper" before the take-off, as the pilot gathered weather data, maps, and forms. From these a flight plan was written, showing the course, altitude, any refueling landings, estimated time of arrival, and alternate courses if the original route had to be abandoned because of unexpectedly bad weather.

Keeping the airplane level and on a chosen course in the air was the simplest part of the WAF's duties. She also had problems of cross-country navigation to solve and resolve as "the mission" proceeded. At her side were large-scale aviation maps which could be used for reference in clear weather, but when clouds hid the ground, the pilot had to navigate by "dead reckoning," computing a compass course from these maps.

Sometimes a WAF navigated by radio alone, if she

were flying a route over which the radio beam was broadcast. A continuous hum indicated that she was on the beam, but any broken note meant she had wandered from her flight path and must make a correction.

As everyone knows, controversy arose in military circles and the Women's Auxiliary Ferry Squadron was disbanded two and a half years after its beginning. But these pilots had already done a splendid job at a time when their country most needed them.

The job the WAFs did in ferrying pursuit aircraft was little short of incredible in view of the prewar theory that most, if not all, women were incapable of handling tricky, high-speed aircraft.

As Nancy says: "In the last year of our existence the WAFs specialized in 'hot' airplanes and delivered more than 50 per cent of the total fighter aircraft ferried by the whole Ferrying Division of the A.T.C. during that time. Imagine the derision I should have received even a few years ago if I had suggested that a woman pilot could ferry a P-51 or P-38. Well, they did—and P-39's at nearly 400 m.p.h. also, to say nothing of other high-speed ships like the P-63's and P-40's.

"The heavy multi-engines were just as adequately handled by WAFs. They flew four-engined, $300,000 Flying Fortresses, as well as B-17's, B-24's, and B-26's. Even the C-54, prewar airliner turned into an army transport, was flown on hundreds of 'missions' by the WAFs.

"All these were ferried by women, with women co-pilots (where necessary)," Nancy adds, "and that is an amazing record! It makes me very proud to be a woman —and to have been associated with such swell, capable girls in an experimental project that was more than successful. Ferrying 'hot' aircraft is certainly not the most peaceful or most 'feminine' occupation."

Nancy did a lot of flying herself during the two and one-half years of the W.A.F.S. activities and, as she says, "got a big kick out of being checked out on all types of airplanes!" The executive side of her activities she considered a necessary and all too time-consuming evil. But although many others also flew airplanes, it is very doubtful if anyone but Nancy Love could ferry planes and still do a fine job in the necessary, though not so pleasant, administrative work too. She had to do two jobs in one!

Nancy sums up her ideas of women's place in the future of aviation. "I feel that women's place in aviation, now that the war is over, will be very important. Aviation has played an increasingly dominant role in American life in the last few years and its future possibilities are limitless. Women pilots in the United States have progressed against great odds compared to the men, for they have had meager opportunities for training. In 1942, for instance, there were only two hundred women with commercial licenses compared to sixteen thousand men, and only twenty-five women with instrument ratings as compared to several thousand men. Today there are two million pilots in this country, men and women, many of whom will continue flying professionally, for a person associated with aviation for a while finds it very hard to return to a less fascinating job.

"There will be plenty of room for skilled women who have been trained in war time aviation and for many more new ones. Women pilots, having proved themselves, will no longer experience the opposition and prejudice of an earlier day."

As for Nancy's personal postwar plans—she wants to encourage more people, particularly women, to fly. She says: "They talk about courage and call flying dare-devilish—that's stupid; flying is simple. Those who have never flown don't realize how safe they are in a plane, those who have know that and want to fly again. I feel that we need a new era in air education, a campaign to teach women that they are safer in a good airplane than in an automobile under normal traffic conditions.

"My goal is to see flying so safe that anybody's grandmother will just naturally take a plane to the sewing club meeting. I want to see flying become as commonplace in our generation as riding a trolley car was in grandmother's day."

Although she temporarily renounced this ambition for the duration of the war, today Nancy Love is again working toward its fulfillment. "In wartime the airplane is primarily an instrument of destruction; in peace it is a means of sport and safe and pleasant transportation.

"I firmly believe that, now the war is over, the small, easy-to-fly, privately owned ship will be a commonplace and women will fly them as a matter of course," Nancy adds. "Any woman can become a pilot who can meet the physical requirements of health and eyesight, has good muscular coordination, ordinary intelligence, and a genuine desire to fly. She can make a profession of aviation if she has the will to endure the hard work that inevitably goes with the acquiring of any skill. Women will fill an important place in the postwar aviation world—and I am sure they will fill it with distinction."

MAXINE MILES

"THE few to whom so many owe so much," as Churchill called the R.A.F., in turn owe much to another few. The ingenuity of Allied engineers and aircraft designers gave these pilots a distinct advantage over their aerial opponents in the early, decisive days of the Second World War.

A few extra oxtanes of gas in British ships that German planes didn't have; a sturdier plane which emphasized longer range and protection for the pilot against an enemy who, caring little for human life, emphasized a maneuverable aircraft which went to pieces at the slightest impact—such little things as these spelled the difference between disaster and victory for the R.A.F. in the air war over Europe!

Maxine Miles (her friends call her "Blossom"), is much more than just another woman at a drawing board in an aircraft plant. As Britain's only woman aircraft designer, she has a clear-cut claim to distinction. As a director of the Miles Aircraft Company, she has been the driving force behind thousands of planes produced for war and peace.

She sits at a drawing board in a glass enclosed office in one corner of the huge aircraft factory. Slim, tallish, dark-haired, dynamic—she bends over a pile of blueprints. Her desk is heaped with factory reports, tracings, and blueprints.

Something catches her eye. She turns to her husband, a slim, boyish-looking man, studying another drawing. "F. G., have you seen this—come have a look." Their heads bend together over the blueprint. This informal conference may save a hundred man hours, install some new safety device in the plant, or design some new wrinkle in an airplane to save a thousand pilot lives.

What a dynamo of energy Maxine Miles is! Her daily routine equals that of any two and a half women you know!

She works twelve hours a day, seven days a week. She can draw a blueprint, work out the wing stress of a plane in a power dive, or figure out the complicated match of fuselage construction.

Blossom calls herself the "odd-job director"—"I have no set pattern for each day, but every day is likely to contain such routine matters as meetings with the personnel manager and interviews with employees who pop into my office for advice and help on their work or private affairs. And, of course, on a particularly busy day there is bound to be an important visitor arriving at the most awkward moment.

"Sometimes I use up a whole day waiting for a plane to be tested. You know the procedure! 9:00 A.M.—aeroplane will be ready to fly at ten o'clock; 10:30 A.M.—aeroplane will be ready in five minutes; 12:30 noon—snags will be dealt with and she'll fly immediately after lunch. Sometimes she does and sometimes she doesn't —but it's always great fun and exciting work."

Blossom is no 'steenth vice-president. She works in close contact with designers and superintends the ex-

perimental department of the corporation—in fact, no
new airplane is produced unless she is there to take
notes. This gives her quite a responsibility!

She teaches the tricky art of draftsmanship to employees at the Technical School (although she never had a
course in the subject in her life). This school, which
gives aeroplane engineering training to boys and girls
sixteen to eighteen, is Maxine Miles' pet project. And
a fine job she has done there too!

"This school is now in its fourth year," she tells us.
"About 120 students come from all over the country to
attend classes, in aircraft drawing, elementary aerodynamics, aircraft materials and specifications. Practical
instruction is given in machine and fitting-shop operations, materials and processes, assembly line and production methods. At the end of their training they can
join our firm or not, as they wish. Most of them do
stay—I'm glad to say!"

A dozen other miscellaneous jobs come her way. She
edits the company magazine, meets with the head of the
welfare department to plan better working conditions
for the employees, and keeps check on the production
of parts in the subfactories of the organization, to
eliminate bottlenecks. During the war, with nightly
bombings of British aircraft factories, these plants were
dispersed into smaller units scattered over the countryside so that no company could ever be completely
knocked out by bombing.

But even all this does not complete her day. She also
runs a home for her husband and two children. She
is definitely the only one of her kind in the world!

She came by her ability honestly. As the daughter of
Johnston Forbes-Robertson, famous actor-manager, and

Gertrude Forbes-Robertson, sister of Maxine Elliott of the American theater, she would be expected to have brains, though not of the mathematical sort. One of her sisters is an actress, the other the wife of the American correspondant, Vincent Sheean.

How did Blossom get into an aircraft plant? It started the day she met Frederick George Miles. Before that time, with a small independent income, she had had no thought of a career.

"I hadn't even given aviation a thought," she says, "but F. G. was already enthusiastically experimenting with a small plane he hoped to build. For years he'd been trying to turn out a practical, low-cost, light-plane."

Her mild interest gradually developed into a real passion for airplanes and anything aeronautical. Soon she was taking flight lessons.

At school Blossom neglected math for painting, and never even took a degree at any of the several schools she attended. Today she knows everything about aircraft except the motors. She says she doesn't even understand the theory of combustion engines, but one thing is sure—in aerodynamics she can hold her own with the best!

After their marriage, Mr. and Mrs. Miles worked together at the Yates airdrome near Bristol. F. G. had been working on a small wooden plane with a wing span of nineteen feet. He foresaw the day in which there would be a big commercial market for a two-seater training plane. A low-winged monoplane was quite an innovation then. Most existing private ships were biplanes or high-winged monoplanes because they were popularly believed to be safer. This Miles plane

was an open two-seater, incredibly light for its size—
one aeronautical journal described it as "the motorcy-
cle of the air."

F. G. had been struggling along with only a small
boy to help him. With marriage he acquired another
helper—and a very competent one too. Blossom spent
all her time, when she was not flying or cooking, helping with the actual construction of the lightplane.
Most of the design and research that went into the first
Miles planes, as well as a major part of the blueprints,
were her work.

One day, the Miles were visiting some friends in
Berkshire. Over the lunch table someone happened to
mention that there was an airfield near Reading struggling against great odds to keep going. The proprietor,
Charles Powis, invited them to build their planes there.
The Reading airport had gasoline pumps and a license
from the Air Ministry as an auxiliary airfield.

"This was just what we needed," Blossom says. "We
knew that as soon as we saw the site. It was close to
two main railroads, with junctions to north and south,
and it also had adequate power and plenty of room for
expansion into neighboring fields."

Everyone was talking about the development of European air transporation, and Blossom could look
ahead far enough to see that this airport might be developed into a terminal for planes from the continent,
as well as for internal British air lines.

The Miles saw the airport on Sunday and by five
o'clock Monday afternoon they owned it. Blossom
added every cent of her inheritance to her husband's
$4,000 capital, and they were now in the aircraft-pro-
duction business—all the way in.

With the way at last clear for development on a larger scale, they got right down to work on their first monoplane. Mr. Miles busied himself with design problems and Maxine made the drawings. As the machine neared completion, everyone within reach was pressed into willing service.

The business, which later grew to be the huge Miles Aircraft Company, started in a very small way. Henry Hill, a woodworker (recently awarded the British Empire Medal for his services to the aircraft industry) was in charge of timber and woodwork. A young boy and Mr. and Mrs. Miles made up the rest of the firm. And always they—F. G. and Maxine Miles—worked together so closely that one writes about them as if they were one person.

Their first enterprise at Reading was the Miles Hawk. It was cheaper to buy and easier to fly than any existing lightplane—a regular sky roadster. They had acquired a number of Cirrus engines at a knock-down price, and they designed a cheap-to-build but sturdy and good-looking two-seater monoplane to fit it.

From the first the Hawk proved to be a best-seller, and in the first year of production alone, more than fifty of them were sold. Orders flowed in for the machine, and, for the next four years, every Miles aircraft had an owner long before it was completed. The organization was constructing custom-built aircraft!

Encouraged by the success of this small plane, Blossom decided to settle down to some serious studying of aerodynamics and drafting, so that she would be really equipped for the career which had originally been thrust upon her but which now she was really into—with all her heart.

She studied aviation designing with typical vigor. "It was one of the most interesting periods of my life," she says. "I discovered that airplanes are very satisfying things, particularly if you help design them yourself."

Mr. Miles tested each new machine as it was completed. Blossom flew with him, taking notes and sharing all the usual dangers of test piloting. If faults were found in a new ship, she dug into the necessary research and discovered how they could be corrected. Sometimes she even took a ship up alone and experimented, with an eye to the tests she had made in the shop. There were days in which she spent eight hours in the air, others when she was busy over a drawing board for just as long.

The Miles went on to design and build more powerful and more highly finished ships. They progressed to King's Cup racers, cabin tourers, twin-engine ships, and finally even to four-engined, feeder-line transports.

By 1935 the company had grown so large that they decided to reorganize and incorporate as a public company to be known as the Phillips-Powis Company (later changed to Miles Aircraft Company). The company now had more than ten types of airplanes on the market. Maxine was put in charge of the drawing office and later made a member of the board of directors. She was the company's contact with the customer as well as its representative with Aircraft Production Ministry officials in London.

A two-seater, high-performance, light airplane capable of long-range flights was made for Col. Charles Lindbergh at one point. It was a Miles Anglo-American Mohawk, a British plane fitted with an American Mesasco Buccaneer engine. It had a distinctive color scheme—black fuselage with yellow wings. Lindbergh maintained that this was easiest to see from the air in case of a forced landing. This was without a doubt the forerunner of the popular "trainer yellow," later widely used for primary training ships in Britain and the United States.

For four years the Miles plant produced only civilian planes. Then a flying school was added to the production plant. The company was given a government contract to train pilots for the R.A.F. reserve. All this plane manufacture plus government contracts brought on a minor boom. The company had by now developed from the original effort in a shed at Shoreham, into one of Britain's leading aircraft manufacturing organizations, a fitting reward for the Miles' years of hard work.

Few people were thinking of war yet, but the Miles felt that the R.A.F. would welcome a training plane that was fast enough to enable a pilot to graduate from it to fighter planes without too much transition difficulty. Such a plane was sorely needed, for, at the time, the R.A.F. was using the United States North American Haruard for this transition, because Britain had nothing that was suitable.

Mr. and Mrs. Miles knew from practical experience and observation the danger of putting a young pilot into the cockpit of a single-seater Spitfire at 300 miles per hour when he had never flown faster than half that speed before. They wanted to produce a dual controlled intermediate fighter-trainer in which a seasoned combat fighter could check out a student, protecting him while doing it. The problem was how to get fighter performance in a two seater!

The Miles Master was the answer. It revolutionized R.A.F. flight-training methods and saved countless pilot lives. It is the fastest trainer in the world. The transition from civilian production to military production was done gradually, as the organization of the defense program in England got under way.

Early in September, 1940, the Battle of Britain opened with terrific aerial dogfights over Southern England and a supply of fighter aircraft greatly needed. Mr. Miles' idea of a simple, all-wooden "utility" fighter which could be mass-produced at a very high rate was submitted to Lord Beaverbrook, then Minister of Aircraft Production.

With characteristic drive, Lord Beaverbrook sponsored the project and gave it every assistance. In nine weeks and two days a twelve-gun fighter took the air.

This high-speed, single-seat fighter had more sustained hitting power and longer range than either the contemporary Hurricane or Spitfire! Considering that it was designed and built under constant threat of air bombing, and that the draftsmen were bombed out of their drawing office while the work was under way, it was really a great achievement. If the Battle of Britain had not been won a few weeks later, it might have been recorded in history alongside the Hurricane and Spitfire.

Throughout the whole of the Second World War there was a continual flow of Miles aircraft designs to meet various needs. They ranged from small pilotless target monoplanes to troop-carrying gliders; from twin-engined fighters and medium bombers to giant six-engined transport monoplanes, designed to carry over 64,000 pounds.

Today the Miles Aircraft Company, which started with two men, a woman and a boy, employs thousands in shop and factories spread all over the countryside. Blossom Miles knows them all personally, making frequent visits to outlying units. The firm has such a fine spirit that it has never been troubled with strikes and it has a record for meeting every demand the government has ever put to it.

Even absenteeism has never been a problem in the Miles Aircraft Company. Blossom says that absentee figures average only 6 per cent—and are that high only in the middle of winter. Considering the difficulties under which the company worked during the war, this is a remarkable record.

"In England all women between the ages of eighteen and forty-five were conscripted for war work in etiher the armed forces, industry, or agriculture," she reminds us. "This means that many of the married women in our company had to work eight and a half hours a day in the plant, then do all their housework and marketing and care for their children. It was a pretty stiff routine, domestic help being entirely unavailable."

The establishment of a day nursery by the company was a big help to many mothers. They could take their children there in the morning and collect them again at night. This not only gave the child expert training and attention but also left its mother with a few free hours for herself.

"This nursery was so well-liked," Blossom adds, "that we are continuing it even now with the war over—by popular demand."

The Miles believe that the best and only way in

which to manage an aircraft manufacturing business is to have complete trust throughout the whole personnel, from the youngest student to the managing director. The Joint Production Board which they set up a few years ago deals with all matters affecting the social well-being of all Miles Aircraft employees.

It is safe to say that no other woman played such an important part in British aviation during the strenuous and critical times from 1928 to 1944 as this vivacious, energetic woman with a young look and a keen interest in people and her work.

The end of the war has not brought any lessening of Blossom's duties, but merely a change in their direction. Her future plans concern quite naturally the welfare of the company and its employees.

"Now that peace is here again, I hope to make all the improvements in this plant we have been unable to touch during the war. We want to build a complete village to house our employees who have been wonderfully patient now for over six years—some billeting in uncomfortable and expensive lodgings, some separated from their families, some sharing houses—others traveling miles to work. We intend to include a hospital, theater, game pavillion, and many similar improvements in our project.

"It is difficult to say what the opportunities for girls in aircraft industries will be in the future of England. We must return to normal before we can tell.

"Since we were not allowed to begin any reconversion plans until after V-E Day and no real work until after V-J Day, we still have far to go to attain prewar conditions of stabilization. During the war years many of our draftsmen were women, all of our machine shops were staffed by women, and our inspection department was largely women. Many of our other departments had as many as 90 per cent women employees. Quite obviously the majority of these will disappear as more and more men return. Some will go back to their old trades, some to their homes. A very few will want to stay and we shall try to fit them in.

"In the higher grades of work, it may be different. In aerodynamics, stress analysis, and aircraft design we have more first-class women who are likely to stay. I believe there will be openings for others of this caliber for many years to come—which probably means permanently."

ELLEN CHURCH

Air Medal
Ellen E. Church
1st Lieutenant Army Nurse Corps
Ninth Troop Carrier Command
September, 1944.
Citation: "For meritorious achievement as flight
nurse while participating in a large number of difficult and dangerous air evacuation missions in
the Mediterranean and European Theaters of Op-
peration. For outstanding skill, determination,
and unswerving devotion to duty in the face of
grave hazards, participating in flights into the
combat zone, where the aircraft was subject to attack from enemy ground installations and hostile
aircraft."

ELLEN CHURCH was the first flying nurse in the European war theater to be awarded the air medal. Being
first is an old habit with Ellen. Fifteen years ago she
was the first airline stewardess in the world, opening up
one of the most popular and interesting jobs in aviation for girls.

Born on a farm, southeast of Cresco, Iowa, Ellen and
her brother had many happy days in a typical rural

school where the three R's were taught diligently, and the older children looked after the little ones.

"I've been interested in medicine ever since I can remember," Ellen recounts. "As a child in the First World War, I knitted wristlets for Belgian refugees. A special treat was permission on Saturdays to fold bandages at the Red Cross. As I proudly sat there, wearing my white headdress with the red cross on it, I wished desperately that I were old enough to be a real nurse. And on the farm, sick and injured animals were always my particular responsibility—any chicken with a broken leg, for instance, was soon sporting a splint."

During her first year in high school, Ellen drove from the farm to school in a horse and buggy. "This meant a really busy day. I was up at 4:30 to go for the cows (the rule being that the cows must be up by sunrise). After I had milked anywhere from four to ten cows, separated the milk, and fed the calves, I fed my horse and myself. Finally he was harnessed and hitched and we started off for school.

"Home again at four in the afternoon, I took care of my horse, brought up the cows, watered and fed the calves. Finally, after dinner, about eight o'clock, I got to my homework. This schedule was varied only by plowing fields or picking crops in season. By the time I was twelve, I was doing a man's work on the farm.

"But it was not all work. We found time to roam the wooded hills, go fishing and on picnics. Our parents were great nature lovers and taught my brother and me all about the animals and birds. I wouldn't have traded my life on the farm for any other. Often in my city life since then I've been homesick for the beautiful sunsets, the smell of the ground in the spring. It was a simple life but a good one."

During her second year in high school Ellen's family moved into Cresco because of her father's illness. Here she had an opportunity to take part in church affairs, join the Campfire Girls, and do her full measure of baby tending.

After graduation, Ellen went to work for an ear, nose, and throat specialist, and learned to assist him in his operations. "I was really only marking time though until the University of Minnesota Nurses Training School opened in September."

After graduation from Minnesota, Ellen was school nurse for a while under the Red Cross in Iowa. Later she became staff nurse at the Desert Sanatorium in Tucson, Arizona. She was in her third job, as instructor of nurses at the French Hospital in San Francisco, learning to fly in her spare time, when she first had the idea that United Air Lines should have nurses as stewardesses on their new eighteen-passenger planes.

All was not well with the air lines in 1930, for in the midst of a depression most people were staying home. And the few who did occasionally travel thought airline fares too high and airplanes still too dangerous. Air-line publicity men pointed out the comforts of air travel, the time and money saved, the safety records—all in vain. Mr. and Mrs. John Doe still took a bus.

Then Ellen Church came along with the idea of air-line salesmanship by stewardesses. "United officials," she says, "at first didn't warm up to having girls in their flight crews. In fact, all but a very few thought it was the silliest thing they'd ever heard of. The concensus of opinion was that there just wasn't any place in aviation for women—and anyhow, they didn't want them."

But a few farsighted officials won out and United Air Lines decided to try Ellen and seven other nurses on its run between Cheyenne and Oakland. The experiment worked so well that what started as an experiment became an American institution, with Ellen Church as its dean. Stewardesses demonstrated their value from a passenger-service standpoint so quickly and decidedly that scores more were employed immediately by the air lines. Today more than 1,500 stewardesses fly the nation's airways and the American air-traveling public has come to take such service for granted. If any salesman is needed today for air travel, the stewardess does the job.

All the air lines wanted stewardesses now that their value had been proven. The job was described in glowing colors to attract nurses to this new adventurous career. The fun of flying, the interesting people a stewardess meets, the travel opportunities and leisure time the job allowed were emphasized.

"Furthermore," air-line officials promised, "you will have to work a maximum of only 110 hours a month. Not only will you have two weeks vacation with pay, but for your vacation traveling you will also be given two round-trip passes between any two cities in the country where air lines operate."

A good salary, sick-leave benefits, and insurance were provided by the air-line companies. All they asked in return was that the applicant be a United States citizen able to meet certain age, weight, and height specifications, and a registered nurse—unmarried!

The "unmarried" qualification proved to be more

of a blight than a blessing to the air lines. The applicant was single when she was accepted for training—
that part was all right—but then after the company had
spent hundreds of dollars on her training, nine times
out of ten she'd marry and leave the air line before
she'd been with the company a month. In self-defense,
the air-line companies made a rule that each girl must
sign a contract saying that if she married before she had
served the air lines a year, she would pay the cost of her
training out of her own pocket. In spite of this obsta-
cle, thousands of girls continued to apply each year for
the job of stewardess. Only twelve out of a thousand
were accepted.

With the coming of war, nurses were so badly
needed on the ground that the air lines no longer required stewardesses to be registered nurses. Girls with
two or more years of college could apply. This offered
a brand new opportunity for co-eds. During the postwar emergency period applications for air hostesses on
some of the major air lines are being accepted from
girls with only one year of college credit plus some
business experience. In a few years the air lines will
undoubtedly swing back to the old requirement of two
years of college or an R.N.

To be an air-line stewardess today one must be between 5 feet 2 and 5 feet 6 and between twenty-one to
twenty-eight years of age, weigh under 125 pounds,
wear no glasses, and be well-mannered; and, as one air
line put it, "We want no glamour."

This hostess of the air must be able to answer a multitude of questions on navigation, meteorology, airplane structures, de-icers, engines, map reading, terrain,

altitude—all of which she is taught in the air-line school.

The first meal eaten in the air was in 1783, when a man and woman went aloft in a balloon and consumed some wine and chicken. Today the stewardess of every one of our domestic air lines can serve a full-course meal to twenty-one people in less than an hour. Air lines spend two million dollars a year on free meals.

A new and interesting opportunity has recently been offered to stewardesses on the huge thirty-passenger, thirty-ton flying boats which make regular trips across the Atlantic. One of the eleven crew members is the stewardess. She must be an R.N., who has had several years' experience with a domestic air line.

It is a very wearing job, sixteen to twenty-five hours on duty with little or no rest. During the trip the stewardess checks passports, prepares formulas for babies, serves three complete meals and makes up berths for sixteen people, to say nothing of possible medical emergencies. No wonder she loses about five pounds on each crossing!

But there are compensations. Each girl makes only two trips a month. She has two or three days in Europe between flights, and two weeks off on her return to the United States. Also, the pay is very good.

Just why do the air lines prefer to have nurses as stewardesses? Ellen Church has been frequently asked. "I feel that a nurse is particularly well fitted for such a position," she answers. "The discipline she gets while in training as a nurse is an excellent background for a stewardess' job. Both positions require poise, tact, and a sound knowledge of human psychology.

"A stewardess must like and understand people, for

her job is a regular laboratory for the study of human nature. She gets so that she can tell pretty well by just looking at people what kind of passengers they will be. Some want attention every minute, some want to be left alone, while others want to eat during the whole trip. Now and then you find someone who wants to wait on you instead.

"She must be able to amuse, to entertain, to converse easily, to anticipate the wants of those entrusted to her care. She must be able to endure weather changes, and adjust herself to unexpected changes in schedule. All these things are part of her day's work. Who has better training than a nurse for such a position?

"There never could be a crisis in a sick room which demanded more self-control than aboard an airliner in trouble. Although most flights are routine and uneventful these days, the stewardess never knows when an emergency may arise. The government has established emergency fields and radio beacons at frequent intervals for safety in air travel on the transcontinental air-line routes. Planes are equipped with two-way radios to keep the pilot in communication with the ground at all times. Weather conditions ahead are relayed to him, and if weather is bad so that continuing the journey would be dangerous, the pilot lands at the closest emergency field.

"It is at such a time that a hostess' real work begins. It is up to her to make her passengers want to continue by air in spite of everything. If she can bring in her full load of passengers after such a delay, feeling that they have gotten more than they paid for, she's done a good job!

"It is a very interesting and many-sided job—a stewardess hears strange tales. I particularly remember one old man traveling from Chicago to Oakland on his first flight. He told how in the early days he had pioneered on horseback all of the country he was now flying over. All night he recorded on postal cards the exact location and the time we passed each place of interest. He was as excited as a child with a new toy."

Ellen Church continued with her job as stewardess for United Air Lines for a year and a half. During that time she traveled more than two million miles by air. After an automobile accident which injured her foot, she returned to the University of Minnesota for additional nursing studies in pediatrics and a B.S. degree in nursing education.

In 1936 she joined the staff of the Milwaukee County Hospital as chief nurse of the children's department. Then, a few years later, she transferred to become director of nurses at the Children's Hospital at Louisville, Kentucky.

As a fitting climax to this variety of medical experiences, Ellen Church entered the Air Evacuation Service of the Army Nurse Corps in 1942. After three weeks of indoctrination at Bowman Field, Louisville, her unit, the 802nd Medical Air Evacuation Transport Squadron, was sent to Morrison Field, West Palm Beach, Florida, for further training and then to North Africa.

The setting is an isolated air base in North Africa. Under the broiling sun, sweaty mechanics start engines on heavily camouflaged army transport planes. Under a wing, the only shade for miles around, an American army nurse in gray overalls is wiping the perspiration from the forehead of a wounded soldier and giving him a drink of cool water.

Suddenly the deep-throated roar of two 1200 horse-power engines warming up shatters the air and shakes the ground beneath her feet. Two stretcher bearers help the nurse place the wounded soldier in the plane's large cabin. Seventeen other wounded men are already on board. The most serious cases are up front where the yaw of the plane is least, the less serious patients in the rear. A flight surgeon makes a last minute check up of the wounded. He looks at the boy who came aboard last.

"Nurse, you'd better give this man some plasma on the way," he says and is gone.

The big transport climbs steadily into the sky. The nurse takes care of the plasma transfusion while a medical technician keeps an eye on the other seventeen men. The morale instilled by the presence of the flight nurse is very great. One boy with a fractured leg smiles weakly—"Gee, a nurse on an airplane. This sure is a streamlined war."

Hours later the huge transport settles down to a smooth landing at an army hospital center behind the lines where ambulances stand waiting.

Not a very exciting trip—this story of an evacuation flight, repeated over and over again in many corners of the earth. But as one army official said: "Nowhere in the inspiring history of nursing has a nobler chapter been written."

To be a flight nurse one must be not over thirty-six, weigh proportionally between 105 and 170 pounds, and be not over six feet in height. Every nurse has to pass the same type of physical examination as an army flyer, and has to be recommended by the senior flight surgeon as being especially qualified for this strenuous service. This is the only branch of duty where women are actually attached to a tactical unit. A rugged two months' course at the Air Evacuation Department of the School of Aviation Medicine at Randolph Field, Texas, follows. The nurses camp out under simulated battle conditions, do guard duty and have gas-mask drills. They practice parachute packing and crash procedure and learn the technique of air ambulance loading and unloading. They study aerial, desert, tropical and arctic medicine, intravenous therapy, field sanitation, and aerial photography before the gold wings are pinned on them.

Even though the war is over, many flight nurses are still at work, transporting wounded back to the United States from former battle areas.

The idea of transporting wounded from battle zone to hospital bases is something new! Air ambulances were used for the first time really in the Second World War—with remarkable results. Only one patient in many thousands died en route. At first many medical people doubted the wisdom of flying certain types of cases with brain and abdominal injuries, but now we know that this is the safest and best method of travel for any wounded serviceman.

Patients reached hospital centers by air not only faster but more comfortably than by any other means of transportation. Compare flying with the rolling of a hospital ship, or the jolting of an ambulance or even a hospital train, and you will see why a plane is so much more satisfactory.

"The pilot and nurse team up to give their passengers the best possible trip," Ellen adds. "We learned to fit the flight to a patient's condition. If we have lung cases aboard, for instance, we fly under ten thousand feet to prevent strain, and the pilot goes out of his way to fly at levels where smooth air prevails."

As many as a thousand men were flown back from base to hospital in a single day. Most of Ellen's thousands of passenger patients had never been off the ground before but she says military wounded are really less trouble than hale and hearty civilians.

"I guess it's because the soldiers expect so little that the least thing we do for them seems wonderful. They're really marvelous—no complaints, no gripes, nothing but cooperation. Even though they're in pain, they act very much like air passengers in peacetime days. The first thing they want to know is whether they are going straight through to New York. Then they want to know how fast we are going, how high we are flying. And finally they start showing pictures of their wives, sweethearts, and youngsters."

The commercial-type planes used for air evacuation of wounded were unarmed. As troop carriers they raced toward battle areas with paratroops and supplies. Being cargo ships, they were not allowed to display the Red Cross symbol of immunity on their return flights with the wounded. These planes were therefore often in very real danger as excellent targets for enemy fighters who had no compunctions about firing on them.

Depending on local conditions, flights usually started from ten to twelve miles behind the front lines, from air strips where all hands sometimes had to dive for fox holes during enemy raids. The trips back to the hospital centers were anywhere from two hundred to five hundred miles, each plane carrying eighteen to twenty-four wounded.

Ellen Church wrote in V-Mail from North Africa: "The country looks much like California, then again like Wyoming. Arabs are underfoot everywhere—colorful to say the least. There is much in our lives that is amusing, and of course equal portions of the opposite. However we seem to thrive on it. We will probably be a bit more streamlined but none the worse for our 'rugged life.'"

When asked whether it's really as hot in Africa as people say, she said: "If you think 135 to 140 degrees is hot, then it's hot. In fact, when our unit was stationed in Tunis, we were quartered in barracks made of wood. Inside the building the heat was stifling. In desperation for sleep, I finally took to sleeping in the grape arbor in the backyard."

All over the Mediterranean areas and western fronts Captain Church kept running across former commercial air-line stewardesses who had volunteered in answer to the call for flight nurses. Some charming air hostess who served you a delicious dinner when you flew from New York to Chicago, might now be a flight nurse, serving blood plasma to a wounded G.I.

"These girls had at first an advantage over nurses who hadn't flown for a living," Ellen says, "because they already had their 'air legs' and felt perfectly at home administering to patients in the air, but it didn't take the others long to become used to working in a hospital plane. And you'd be surprised at how many flight nurses there are whose chief ambition is to be an air-line stewardess now that the war is over."

After many months in North Africa and Sicily, Ellen

was finally ordered to report for a special assignment at a training base in England. Now having six stars on her campaign ribbon, Ellen passed on to other nurses preparing for D-Day the military air-evacuation experience she had accumulated in ninety thousand miles of ambulance flights.

Just before the war ended, Captain Church was assigned as instructor of flight nursing at the A.A.F. School of Aviation Medicine at Randolph Field. There she helped train many of the flight nurses who are now still overseas.

"Once my army responsibilities are over, and I'm a civilian again, I hope to get back in the air, maybe on an air line, or in some private concern—I've already been offered both types of jobs. I'd like to tour the whole United States by air from coast to coast and Canadian border to the Gulf. I never seem to get enough of air travel."

HELEN HARRISON

VANCOUVER-BORN Helen Harrison is probably less well-known in her own country than in any other English-speaking country in the world. Perhaps this is because she is more cosmopolitan than Canadian. Her exceptional aviation record in many parts of the world is something for Canadians to be proud of. Her fine work breaking down barriers of prejudice against Canadian women in flying jobs entitles Helen to a top-ranking place in aeronautical circles.

As the first military aviatrix in the world, with flying licenses in four countries, this forthright young woman has a record that would turn many a male pilot green with envy. One reporter ran this article on her recent return to Canada:

"Man's last vestige of superiority (put that down lady, you'll like this) walked resignedly to the open window and jumped out when First Officer Helen Harrison, just returned from flying R.A.F. planes with the A.T.A. in England, walked into the room. It's just as well that 'man's last vestige' didn't wait around for details or he'd have done a much grimmer job on himself.

"Her conversation ran something like this: 'the Mosquito is my favorite bomber, of course; I like to call it a Spitfire bomber—that Spit's a dream—it's the best fighter I guess, but I like the American Mustang too—that Mosquito though, I had it doing 350 level and it didn't flatten out.'

"An effervescent, very personable young woman was talking about the planes she had flown overseas—forty-nine different types of aircraft is her record (everything except a four-motored bomber). She has half a million hours in her log book!

" 'We used an Anson to taxi people around at times, and one day one of our girl pilots flying it met a twin-engined German bomber. It fired a burst at them—' Helen hesitated with a look of mischief in her eye, the audience leaned forward expectantly—'and scared the dickens out of them,' she concluded! Some girl!"

How one blonde, blue-eyed, vivacious Canadian girl could pile up such a record in her brief span of years is quite a story.

It all started when Helen was nine. Her grandfather left a legacy and the Harrisons decided they should travel. Helen has been traveling ever since. From Canada to England, and from England to Belgium she was transplanted, finally completing her formal education in Belgium. This early voyaging must have left its mark, for when Helen came of age and stepped out on her own, she was able to call "home" wherever she hung her helmet and goggles—a valuable asset for any pilot.

She was soon used to the huge clippers and airliners as a convenient means of transportation, but it was several years before she made her first small-plane "joy-hop." Quite by chance, she was roped into aviation as a career.

She and another girl made a week-end trip to a seaside resort in England. While there, Helen took a hop at the local airport just as thousands of others have done since the earliest barn-storming days. But this time the small injection took.

The flying urge was instilled in Helen and she was determined to become a pilot. Before this time she had been training for the job of beautician, but now the idea grew on her, as her flying lessons progressed, that being a hairdresser was a pretty tame job compared with the possibility of a flying career. But her savings were rapidly disappearing, and this was not a day in which flying jobs for women were lying around loose all over Canada, so Helen hesitated to sink her whole future into something so insecure. She qualified for her "A" license after only six and three-quarters hours of instruction—an unusual feat in itself, since the majority of women students take ten or more. Her family, in sympathy with her flying aims, helped her to buy a small plane.

Now the time had arrived to make some final decision about this flying business—but the decision had really been made for her. Flying was in her blood to stay, and there was no turning back. She was going to make a living out of it—or else!

Helen traded in her first ship for a Fox Moth and later, the Moth for a four-passenger Falcon, earning her way to a higher license by hopping passengers. Soon England, to which she had returned, became too small a country for someone with her traveling heritage. Other countries invited exploration. She flew her ship across the channel to France and down to Marseilles, then leaving it there, she went by boat to

Singapore, where she did quite a bit of seaplane flying.

The hours piled up in her logbook, and with such a variety of flying experience Helen began looking for a more definite, tangible contribution to make to aviation.

After thoroughly examining all flying possibilities, Helen decided her best opportunity was in South Africa, where a government pilot-training program was being contemplated to build up a reserve air force. Helen made the long trip to Cape Town but when she arrived found that although flying jobs were available, more flying hours were required for a commercial pilot's license there than in England. Her total flying time qualified her to take the examination for a commercial license in England, but almost a hundred more hours were needed to apply for the same certificate in South Africa. So she returned to England to pile up more time.

She first passed her commercial written examination, and, having sold her Falcon, bought another ship, a Spartan, for the "joy ride" trade, operating near Portsmouth for several months. She went up for her instructor's permit next, and successfully passed the exam, becoming the second woman flight instructor in England.

Helen returned to South Africa with the necessary additional hours, arriving at a very good time. The government of the Union of South Africa had just decided to go ahead with a pilot-training course, and intended to train a thousand pilots for reserve duty within the next three years. Although friends "pooh-poohed" the idea of a woman having any chance for a position as instructor, Helen applied, demonstrated her flying ability, and got the job. Her duties were to train reserve candidates in flying and ground school.

She was the first woman instructor to work in South Africa. Additional instruction work for civil aviation was added to her schedule at Grahamstown, Johannesburg, and Pretoria, the capital of the Union. A few days each week she flew into the Orange Free State from Johannesburg, a distance of about 150 miles, to conduct a flying school. Helen was now a regular flying "school marm"!

Flying conditions in South Africa were quite different in many ways from those in either England or the United States. Fields for refueling were few and far between. The plane carried wireless telephone equipment, but the radio stations contacted were not many and the reception of signals difficult owing to constant heavy static.

There were no lighted airways for night flying, no well-equipped landing fields operated by the government. Pilots were dependent on their own ability for navigating as the radio range beacon is entirely absent in Africa. Just to make an already difficult condition more difficult, the weather was rather variable. Pilots had a lot of trouble with head winds.

The ground presented problems for forced landings too. "For example," Helen says, "one might approach a field that looked good from a height of a thousand feet but upon closer examination would prove useless. Ant hills caused the trouble. Not the little sandy pockmarks we call ant hills, but clay domes, three feet high, baked as hard as bricks by the hot sun. A plane landing and striking such hills would be a washout for fair. And the ants living in them can whip their weight in tigers."

In her many flights over the South African veldt, Helen had no real accident, but she remembers one rather bad day. Forced down by a terrific head wind, she landed at a small refueling field liberally covered with thick growing brush. Taking off again later, these bushes tangled in her landing gear, almost throwing the ship, but she managed to get off safely.

Helen was trying to reach Cape Town before dark but had lost so much time she was afraid she wouldn't make it. A landing would have to be made without light, for the fields down there, even in such large towns as Cape Town, do not burn runway lights throughout the night. Floodlights are turned on only for ships which have telephoned in the time of their arrival. The field crew was not expecting Helen to arrive after dark.

To add to her difficulties, she had to climb the plane over mountains to reach Cape Town. She was forced to climb eleven thousand feet to clear the obstructing peaks, although her cruising altitude had been eight thousand feet. Because of the brush on the landing gear, it was all the ship could do to make the climb.

She approached the field with some apprehension, prepared to find it dark and deserted. She gritted her teeth and side-slipped, wondering if her career were to end in the next few minutes. Then the miracle happened. The lights of the field blinked on. First the runway markers, then the huge landing flood lights. Helen's heart dropped from her throat to its normal resting place—and she set the ship down neatly onto the runway. Later she learned that the lighting had

been for another plane. This pilot phoned in from out
of town to cancel his lighting instructions a few minutes after Helen landed. She had arrived just in time.

Helen enjoyed this South African government
course very much because it was so intensive it kept
her flying up to par. In addition to giving instruction,
she occasionally took part in flying exhibitions too, an
item in the *South Africa Airnews* tells us.

"Miss Harrison is one of the most skillful stunt pilots
in this country. Only a few weeks ago her turn at
Baragwnath during a show arranged in honor of the
film stars, Bebe Daniels and Ben Lyons, was one of the
highlights of the program. Her inverted flying was one
of the most polished features of the exhibition."

The longest flight Helen ever made was a 4,500-mile
hop from Cape Town to Cairo, which she says provided her with far less excitement than her first camel
ride. Not all her African flights, however, were dull.
Once, flying a military doctor over the African veldt,
she found herself way off her course. Later she discovered that the physician's electrical equipment in his
instrument case had thrown the compass off.

Out of gas and lost, she picked out a relatively
smooth stretch of ground near a native village and
gingerly set the ship down. It rolled to a bumpy stop
and immediately natives ran out, chattering and making wild motions with their arms, obviously very excited. Neither Helen nor the doctor could make the
natives understand that they just wanted to know
where they were. Finally one native was found who
understood a little English. Helen showed him the
map and explained their predicament. He nodded,
snatched the map from her and ran off as hard as he

could go. The natives stood around, grinning, obviously waiting for his return.

Before long an ancient car was seen bumping along the ground toward them. Out stepped the local missionary who showed them their position on the map. He provided gasoline which had to be strained through a silk handkerchief into a can. Then Helen lugged the eight-gallon can up to the opening on top of the ship and poured the fuel in.

While Helen was in South Africa, a women's auxiliary air force was formed, which became popular at once and grew to quite a size. At the same time Helen learned from Australian acquaintances that a similar women's flying organization was being formed in Australia.

So she was pleased, upon her return to England, to find that similar civil air guard training was proceeding enthusiastically there, at flying rates of two shillings and six pence an hour (about sixty cents in United States money). Helen spent four months in England training men and women pilots for the civil air guard, then decided it was time to go home to Canada. She discovered that her mother and father were now living in Virginia, so she stopped off in the United States for a while on the way. She made good use of her stay there by taking out her United States commercial pilot's license.

Helen was amazed to find how much less air-minded the United States was than other countries in which she had flown. Great Britain and South Africa had been subsidizing flying clubs for some time, making it possible for people of small means to take up flying.

Almost as soon as she arrived in Canada, Helen began to take an active part in the defense program there. She landed an instructor's job at Cub Aircraft, Limited, in Hamilton, where she broadened her already extensive experience by flying lightplanes.

At the outbreak of the war she transferred to the Kitchener Flying Club. Once again she was training air-force pilots. As assistant instructor she helped turn out P.O.P.'s (pilot officers provisional) for the R.C.A.F.

"If they didn't like a woman instructor, they didn't show it. I was the first one these military pilots had ever had. I got on very well with my men students, but of course—" she grinned, "they were under military discipline and couldn't very well object."

One reporter interviewing Helen after her return to Canada, said:

"She believes that her presence in the officers' mess here may force young Canadians to take up the study of Iroquois, or Eskimo.

"'When I was associated with the officers in South Africa, the colonel one day asked how it came about that so many of the young officers were displaying an interest in Afrikaans, the Boer language,' she recalled. 'No one seemed to know, until at last one officer admitted that they couldn't very well swear in English in front of a woman.'"

After her term there was finished, she went to Toronto and offered herself to the Air Force for a still more active part in the war effort. Months of interviews with Ottawa officials followed; and, like many other frustrated patriots, Helen arrived exactly nowhere. The Air Force refused to recognize her status, evidently because she wore skirts, when she said she wanted to instruct army pilots or ferry military planes in Canada.

Although somewhat disillusioned, Helen didn't let this rebuff get her down. She decided that if she couldn't get in the "front door" she'd try the back. Her idea to form a women's flying class was snapped up by Bob Redmayne's flying school, and she went to work as an instructor again, concentrating on attracting women to the school.

Her women's class grew in two months to twenty-five members, with inquiries flooding in from several hundred more, most of whom were interested, but not financially able to take the course. These twenty-five fledglings came from many corners of the country. One was a school teacher, another a stenographer, still another a worker in a radio-parts factory. One was a commercial parachute jumper.

Most of the girls took flying in easy doses agreeing with their pocketbooks—half an hour a week. At this rate they wouldn't be qualified for any practical air job in less than two years. But what Helen hoped to do was to form a Women's Auxiliary Air Force, like those operating in Australia, England, and South Africa. She hoped to link up with influential women war-service workers who could boost the movement along. By direct appeals to wealthy individuals and to firms which could supply the necessary aircraft, equipment, headquarters, uniforms, and other essentials she hoped to train a group of capable women pilots for ferrying work.

By service to their country during the war these girls hoped to secure a Canadian "women's suffrage" of the air. They wanted to establish once and for all that skirts are no barrier to a woman who is out to make a career for herself in commercial flying.

But the idea of a Women's Auxiliary Air Force in Canada never quite jelled, so when the opportunity came, Helen jumped at the chance to join Jacqueline Cochran's group of women pilots going to England to ferry planes for the R.A.F.

Some time later a Canadian newspaper quoted Helen's first impression of the group. " 'Every one of us one hundred A.T.A. girls would jump at the opportunity of flying planes in action. If the Russian girls can do it, we can too. If women are called for combat pilots, there will be a rush to get the job,' declared First Officer Helen Harrison, Air Transport Auxiliary ferry pilot, just home on furlough after sixteen months in Britain. The first Canadian woman flyer to join that organization, she has a flight instructor's rating in four countries and has flown thirty-two different types of aircraft while a ferry pilot in Britain.

" 'There is no likelihood of women making up air crews and going into action,' she said, 'but we girls often discuss it. Personally, I'd like to fly a Mosquito bomber. I have ferried several of them.

" 'It's an interesting job, ferrying planes. There's always a certain challenge, a big responsibility. A huge bomber, perhaps, has to be brought safely to an operational base. We need sound judgment for the ferry flying job, for we do not use instruments.

" 'We have to do our own navigation, and as we don't use radio we have to use our own judgment. So we don't fly when the ceiling is at eight hundred feet or when visibility is less than two thousand yards. After

all, there are barrage balloons to cope with,' the pilot
pointed out.

" 'We get up about 8 A.M., on our jobs here, have
breakfast and take a bus to the airdrome. Then we
pick up our 'chits,' or assignments. Then we check on
the weather, find a taxi plane to transport us to some
plane factory where we are to collect a plane for delivery.' "

Helen says she never encountered enemy aircraft
while ferrying a plane. In fact, she never saw a Nazi
plane at any time but admits she did have one narrow
escape—not because of enemy action however.

"I had to make a crash landing, hitting the ground
at 110 miles an hour. The plane was nose heavy because of faulty ballast conditions. The plane was dam-
aged, and I was shaken up and suffered from shock, but
after a night in the hospital I was back on the job next
day."

Ferry pilots in most cases, fly alone. They usually
wear regular uniform jacket and slacks while on the
job. When they fly single-seaters, however, the hood
must be opened in taking off or landing, so they add
coveralls, goggles, and helmet to their attire.

An A.T.A. pilot has to have a lot more know-how
than the average military pilot who is checked out on
one type of aircraft and seldom flies another kind.
Helen might have to jump from Taylorcraft to Spitfire
to Wellington, to Mitchell—all in one day. There is a
bit of suspense and excitement she says when a new
type of aircraft appears, knowing one might be called
upon to ferry it somewhere on a moment's notice without previous instruction.

"One simply had to take off, flying with the book of

instructions on the particular aircraft in one's lap, and hope she could find the right gadgets at the right time."

Her greatest thrills while in England came, not in the air, which was a relatively routine procedure, but when on leaves to London where she sometimes met a Canadian flyer, now a seasoned veteran, whom she had taught to fly.

Helen believes that there is a great future for women in flying; for she thinks that, being more sensitive than men, they are better fitted to control the delicate machinery of a flying craft. She should know!

Now that Canada is no longer at war, Helen has taken a job as demonstrator for a British aircraft company. This concern is shipping airplanes across the Atlantic to her. She flies from city to city throughout Canada, demonstrating these ships to the public.

"I am starting with a four-place, single-engined Proctor, but later will do some demonstration of twin-engined planes also. My specific job is to bring this company's planes before the Canadian public and demonstrate to them what really fine ships they are.

"The future for women pilots in Canada is, I believe, definitely brighter now that the war is over. It is entirely up to the individual girl herself, of course, to make her opportunity in aviation. Each one must find an opening and convince the aircraft manufacturer or airport owner that she can do the job. But I think there should be many openings for women as instructors, first of all—and after they have gained enough experience, more advanced jobs as demonstrators."

Demonstrating airplanes is one field where women have a definite advantage over men because of the psychological factor of a woman handling a plane. The average man or woman seeing a woman pilot at the controls says: "This must be a safe, easy-to-fly plane when a woman can pilot it. If she can do it, I can!" Regardless of the facts, this is the public reaction, and more and more manufacturers, particularly those who make light sport planes and family planes, will realize as time goes on that a woman demonstrator furnishes valuable sales psychology which helps to put over a product.

CAROLINE IVERSON

THE Douglas transport, its four 1,200-horsepower engines wide open, left the runway with an earth-shaking roar. Newfoundland faded away below as the huge army ship turned its nose toward Greenland. Aboard the C-54 were twelve journalist and radio notables, invited by the Air Transport Command on a two-week trip to visit its North American bases at Newfoundland, Greenland, Iceland, and Labrador.

The white-capped Greenland mountains, towering ten thousand feet above the horizonless expanse of arctic winter, reached majestically upward to welcome these guests, as the silver ship swooped down to a landing. Important figures of the news world stepped out of the opening in the plane's side into a 30° below zero world: dapper Carl Levin, of the *Herald Tribune;* mike-carrying Dave Driscoll, of Mutual; John Tyrell, of *Newsweek;* Frank Cipriani, of the Chicago *Tribune;* and Dinty Moore, fast-writing United Press man. Then, talking to Bob Considine, of the International News Service, best known for his ghost writing of Ted Lawson's *Thirty Seconds Over Tokyo,* a slim young woman stepped out, looking trim and smart in her war-correspondent's uniform. This single woman in the group was Caroline Iverson, aviation editor of *Life* Magazine.

"I sure have had a lot of luck!" Caroline says, but it took more than good luck to make her, at twenty-seven, aviation editor of the world's most important pictorial magazine, sent to Greenland as *Life's* special correspondent.

She was lucky, of course, to be born into a family rich on both sides in literary ability and journalistic achievement, but the many breaks which came her way, through crowded years of experiences rivaling an *Arabian Nights* tale, would have meant nothing if Caroline hadn't had the initiative and intelligence to make the most of every opportunity.

It was her own self-confidence, not luck, that created her first job when, fresh out of college, she persuaded the reluctant editor of a small-town local paper that he needed a shopper's column and that she was the one to write it. And it was hard work, not chance, that made this job the initial rung on a ladder by which she has climbed to her present success.

Today, as aviation editor of *Life,* Caroline has found the perfect blending of her two greatest interests. Her interest in aviation is an acquired taste, but her journalistic leanings were inherited, for as Caroline says herself: "I was literally brought up on a newspaper."

Her father has been in newspaper work ever since he left school at the end of the ninth grade to become a printer's devil on the Duluth, Minnesota, *Tribune.* Today he is make-up editor of the Milwaukee *Journal,* rated as one of the ten best papers in the country.

The Iverson home was always full of newspaper talk; it colored all their lives. Caroline and her year-younger sister, Dorothy, were constantly listening to stories of the newspaper world brought home by their father—interesting incidents of his work, behind-the-scenes tales of people in the news, problems of getting out a good newspaper day after day.

Mrs. Iverson added her quota, too, to Caroline's literary heritage. She had grown up with a strong interest in literature and had majored in English at the University of Wisconsin. She graduated with a Phi Beta key and was a teacher for three years before she married. Mrs. Iverson exposed her children at a very early age to all the childhood classics, read aloud to them from the *Odyssey* and *Iliad,* and fed Caroline liberal doses of creative writing as well.

"Mother first put me to work writing poetry to keep me out of mischief while I was home sick with the measles," Caroline recalls. "Since I subsequently had all the other children's diseases, one after another, I managed to fill a whole notebook with childish rhymes. My third-grade teacher sent a few of these to the Chicago *Daily News,* and for the first time I saw my name in print!"

Despite this eight-year-old taste of a by-line, Caroline Iverson was no child prodigy. Her parents were too sensible to develop only her mind and neglect the development of a healthy body. The family lived on the outskirts of Wauwatosa, a suburb of Milwaukee, Wisconsin. Summers the children spent entirely out of doors where there were plenty of trees to climb, grapevines to slide down, and a river to swim in. At the age of four, Caroline had been doing a fair imitation of the breast stroke, thanks to Mrs. Iverson who had been a swimming instructor at college.

Caroline's interest in both sports and writing developed more fully during her high-school years. She was girls' sports editor of the high-school newspaper and editor-in-chief of the yearbook.

Caroline confesses that she was socially backward in high school, but adds: "When I got to the university, I blossomed out so suddenly during my first semester that I almost flunked. Out coking or dancing nearly every night in the week, I seemed determined as only a college freshman can be not to let my work interfere with my pleasure."

Her conscience soon caught up with her, however, and she settled down to work. From the start, at the University of Wisconsin in Madison, journalism-education was her major—journalism because she loved it and education because her mother had warned her that a teacher's certificate might be a good thing to have to fall back on. This was right in the middle of the depression of the thirties.

Sophomore journalism at Wisconsin not only involved analyzing good writing in metropolitan newspapers from all over the country, but also included regular assignments on Madison's daily newspapers. Caroline covered countless P.T.A. meetings and such, which she admits rarely rated much newspaper space, but were fun to do. Now and then she helped to rewrite stories for the society editor. This resulted in her taking over the society desk during her senior year for one hectic week end. Although her male associates offered all kinds of assistance, Caroline stayed up all night, writing headlines, laying out pages, and trying to get stories ready for the Sunday section.

Caroline's courses in journalism at Wisconsin covered just about everything a beginner on a small newspaper might be called upon to do—reporting, advertising copy writing, movie and theater reviews, and even a few editorials.

"Helen Patterson's course in special-feature writing gave me my first real boost into journalism, I think," Caroline says. "In it we learned to analyze magazines thoroughly and then try to write something that one of them might buy. It was just the stimulus I needed to start free-lancing. Also, since part of the course was to work out a job project (selling some service to a luke-warm prospective employer), I developed a 'Shopper's Column' which eventually got me my first job after college."

That was with the Janesville, Wisconsin, *Daily Gazette,* where Caroline reported for duty in the advertising department. During the next six months it was literally the butcher, the baker, and the candlestick-maker—plus the hardware store man, the shoemaker, and the ladies dress shop manager who became Caroline's friends. They were the ones to whom she sold space in her weekly column of "advertising in a chatty way."

She wrote a daily fashion column too, which she says "was a big thing for me to take on, considering that I had never had any training nor even any real interest in clothes." Aileen Ryan, fashion editor of the Milwaukee *Journal,* when appealed to for a little advice on how to get started, gave some that was brief and to the point: "Subscribe to the New York publication, *"The Women's Wear Daily,* and just use common sense." And so Caroline's fashion column was launched.

One day, the *Gazette* managing editor, hearing that Clarence Chamberlin, the famous flyer, was barnstorm-

ing the country to interest people in aviation and selling rides to the public thirty miles away in Rockford,
Illinois, sent Caroline over to get a story about him.
She not only got her story but flew back to Janesville
leaning over his shoulder in the cockpit, watching the
dials on the instrument panel. That was her first taste
of the flying that was to make such a change in her life.

Caroline ran her shopper's column, wrote her by-
lined fashion text, and dabbled lightly in various radio
broadcasts, theater-reviewing, and display-advertising
accounts. At one time she was even commentator for
a $10,000 fashion show at a near-by summer resort.

"You know," she says, "that's one of the advantages
of working on a small-town paper. All kinds of opportunities are thrust at you. On a big-city paper you have
to show genius, particularly if you're a woman, not to
be lost in the shuffle. Any girl who wants to get into
the newspaper game should start near home on a small
paper and make a reputation for herself there—then
the big papers will come to her."

Then one day Caroline's advertising boss called her
into his office. "Sit down, Caroline," he said, looking
very sheepish.

She sat down beside his desk, suspecting nothing—
and then the blow fell.

"I'm afraid we're going to have to let you go!" he
said. Caroline looked at him incredulously. This just
wasn't possible. She knew she had been doing a good
job. This same man had told her so just the week before.

"I'm terribly sorry," he said. "You've been doing
fine work, but we have to reduce our budget and let

part of our staff go. You're one of the newest recruits, so you have to go."

"And that," says Caroline, "is one of the disadvantages of working on a small-town paper."

It didn't take her long to get another job. The Milwaukee *Journal* soon offered her a position in its advertising department. "It was not a very glamorous job," Caroline says reflectively; "it consisted mostly of selling ads over the phone."

Since this job, though good experience, was not very exciting, Caroline began to look around for an outside interest. She had been working at the job only six months when she read in the paper that the government was going to give a Civilian Pilot Training Program at the university. She had been wanting to learn to fly ever since that flight with Chamberlin and, as a graduate of the university, she thought she might be eligible for this program. One of those lucky breaks she has had so often, came to her rescue now; and, under a quota of one girl to fifteen men allowed, she found herself the one girl selected for this group.

Every morning she was at the airport at six, had her flight lesson, and was back in town to begin work at nine. Seven to ten each evening was spent at ground school studying navigation, meteorology, and civil air regulations. It was quite a grind, but she loved it!

For a girl who was later to pilot a plane to Mexico and Alaska and to fly to Greenland and Iceland, her first flight was anything but an auspicious occasion. She was nervous and excited, and much to her horror her stomach rebelled and she was airsick.

"In fact," she says, "I was such a bad student that after a few flights my first instructor refused to teach me any longer. That proved to be another lucky break for me, really, because I was given a new instructor who was truly wonderful. I know now that except for his patient instruction I would never have completed the course."

"Teach," as she called him, was a natural-born pilot but so very inarticulate that he had been unable even to write his written test for an instructor's rating, so he was giving flight instruction now only by special permissoin of the local Civil Aeronautics Authority inspector. Caroline helped "Teach" complete his written exam (which at that time was of the long essay type rather than the multiple-choice test given today). It must have been quite amusing to see the veteran pilot depicting by hand movements his answers to the test, while his only girl student wrote them down in readable form. He passed the test!

Caroline says she certainly was not a natural pilot, but adds: " 'Teach' encouraged me and babied me through when I was ready to give up." It was a great satisfaction to both of them when Caroline sailed easily through her written and flight exams.

Getting into the secondary C.P.T. program was another piece of good fortune. The university was having trouble filling its quota for the secondary program, which consisted largely of advanced maneuvers and acrobatics in an open Waco biplane. So, although at first the authorities had definitely said "No girls!" they decided to admit Caroline after all. Knowing that she couldn't manage the stiff flight-training program and her job too, Caroline decided to resign from the newspaper.

"That was the toughest program I have ever undertaken in my life," Caroline said. "Engines and aircraft were particularly difficult subjects for me, and I'm sure glad I had a strong foundation of mathematics, or I really would have been sunk. I just worked my head off for three months—didn't have a single date.

"There were nineteen boys in the group, though," she grinned, "and I was the only girl, so we had lots of fun on bad-weather days when there was no flying, having cokes and dancing to the airport juke box."

After the C.P.T. program was finished, Caroline took examinations for ground-instructor ratings in navigation, civil air regulations, and meteorology. Before long she was teaching these subjects three nights a week to a class of fifty people at the local high school. In between she wrote articles about the town's airport activities for the local paper.

A few months later the C.A.A. inspector recommended her for the job of C.P.T. ground-school instructor at Carroll College near by, and she conducted classes there one night a week. And as if she didn't already have enough to do, she asked the director of the Wisconsin University C.P.T. program if she could teach ground-school subjects to his group. He told her that if she would be his publicity director for that semester, he would arrange for her to have the ground-school job the next semester. Caroline accepted his offer.

By now she had four distinctly different jobs and was taking the apprentice-instructor course, which followed the secondary under the C.P.T., all at the same time. Later she also taught meteorology one night a week at the Milwaukee School of Engineering, the first woman to teach there since the First World War.

One day at a state Civil Air Corps breakfast flight, Caroline learned from an army officer that licensed women flyers had a national organization called the Ninety-Nines. She wrote to a friend of the officer who was a member, Teddy Kenyon, about the possibility of membership and received a very cordial letter in reply, inviting her to the annual convention a few weeks later at Albuquerque.

So Caroline and a friend, Maggie Seip (who was later killed while on duty with the W.A.S.P.) headed for Albuquerque in a borrowed Taylorcraft plane. Neither of them had ever flown outside Wisconsin before; Caroline had 120 hours, Maggie about 50, but Caroline was good at navigation, so off they started.

The weather was terrible. They encountered storms all the way and were constantly delayed by fog. The only extra equipment in the fragile lightplane was a portable radio so they flew all the way to Albuquerque on its beam.

At Kansas City, where they were held up because of a low ceiling, they met a Boston woman, also headed for the convention. She however, was flying an instrument-equipped Fairchild 24 and had an instrument rating in her logbook. She left the two girls with many misgivings and went on ahead to the convention. Once there she had everyone agitated with an account of "those two inexperienced girls flying cross country with almost no equipment!" Two days later, Caroline and Maggie calmly landed at Albuquerque, as if they had just flown over from a near-by field.

The convention was very exciting to them and they especially enjoyed meeting so many women pilots from different parts of the country. The trip back was as uneventful as the one down had been eventful, and they arrived at Wauwatosa in three days, thanks to strong tail winds. Before long Wisconsin had its own chapter of the Ninety-Nines with Caroline as its first president, and breakfast flights around the state to visit members were prize Sunday morning fare.

One of Caroline's former students had purchased a brand new de luxe Taylorcraft while Caroline was at Albuquerque, and on her return they flew all over the state together, building up flying experience.

One day she and Gene (the owner of the Taylor-craft) decided it would be fun to take a trip to Nevada to visit his cousin, and from there to go on to visit Caroline's sister in Seattle. When they reached Seattle, they decided that Alaska was just a stone's throw away, a mere fifteen hundred miles, so they might as well take in that trip too!

Just about every complication possible came their way on this trip. Airports were few and far between (this was before the U.S. Army built its network); the mountains, topped by McKinley's 23,000 feet, were not even indicated on their maps. They had water in their gasoline, several forced landings because of bad weather; they ducked around, over, and through un-expected storms. Over a wild part of Wyoming they ran low on gas. Spotting a lone man, they swooped dangerously low to shout, "Where can we land this thing?" The man pointed, of all places, up to a pla-teau—the emergency landing field in Knight, Wyo-ming, and the highest field in the United States—7,600 feet above sea level.

To these two this was "The Supreme Adventure" and all such set-backs merely part of the game. Caroline called it "the high spot of my life," little dreaming of the many higher spots to follow.

Caroline received quite a lot of publicity during the trip as a result of a request for day-to-day coverage for the Associated Press. Consequently, the next year she found herself giving talks at civic gatherings on the average of once a week, besides her teaching and publicity work.

The following spring, *Life* Magazine sent a scout to universities in the Middle West to unearth writing talent. The School of Journalism at the University of Wisconsin must have recommended Caroline, because out of the clear blue sky, a letter arrived one day offering her the possibility of a staff job with *Life*.

Caroline didn't jump at this opportunity, as you might expect she should. She was happy where she was, and the mere thought of living in New York frightened her. It was her Dad's urging that finally persuaded her to go to Chicago for an interview. Mary Fraser, *Life's* representative, did much, Caroline said later, to influence her decision, for her pleasant personality and kindness made working for *Life* seem very desirable. Then, too, Caroline realized that such a job would combine her two greatest interests, journalism and aviation.

Another letter from *Life,* suggesting that she try the job for the summer, finally made up her mind. She didn't have anything planned for the summer—all her present work ended with the school year, and a summer in New York certainly sounded like fun!

"After I had accepted the job of aviation researcher for *Life* Magazine for the summer of 1942, I flooded New York with letters," Caroline reminisces. "I was in a dither, and I asked *Life* everything from what to wear in New York to where I should live and how I should get to work. I even wrote to the Chamber of Commerce for subway schedules, and to all the hotels for possible accommodations."

Arriving at *Life* with a lot of big ideas—which, she says rather ruefully, were soon knocked out of her—Caroline soon swung into the routine of a large publication. Her greatest struggle was in learning to think entirely in terms of picture stories. Before long, however, she was completely sold on the idea.

In the fall of 1942 a telegram arrived from Jacqueline Cochran which threatened to cut short Caroline's affiliation with *Life,* for the war's duration at least. It read: "If you are interested in women's flight training for ferrying duty with American Air Corps, qualifications 200 hours certified flying time, age 21 to 35 years, equivalent of at least high school education, I will be available for appointments, New York City, September 21st and 22nd. If accepted after personal interview and you pass army physical, remuneration will be 150 dollars monthly while training and 250 monthly on ferrying duties."

Caroline was not at all anxious to give up her new job, but with the country at war, she felt it her duty to join this group, which later became the W.A.S.P. She went for an interview with Miss Cochran, passed the army physical, and then informed *Life* that she was leaving. They were startled. Caroline didn't know it at the time, of course, but they were sending the current aviation editor to the Pacific and planned to have her take over his job.

She was torn between two duties. She felt that she

had a strong personal obligation to offer her services as a pilot to the government because of the extensive free training she had received. But on the other hand, *Life* told her there would be no one left in the aviation department if she left. "After all," *Life* argued persuasively, "our close work with the Army and Navy, keeping the public informed of what goes on in a world conflict, is war work too."

On advice of the commanding general of the Flying Training Command, Caroline agreed to stay until they had found someone to take her place. But *Life* never did find anyone, so Caroline gave up all idea of joining the W.A.S.P.

She had been working for *Life* about five months when one morning two of the editors walked into her office on the thirty-first floor of the Time and Life Building in Rockefeller Center and said without any preamble: "We'd like you to go to Texas tonight to do a story on the *Suzy Q*, the airplane with a personality."

The next day Caroline was having lunch with the crew of the *Suzy Q*, but in Washington instead of Texas—the crew had suddenly changed location. Major Felix Hardison, commander of the chip, a tall, lanky Oklahoman, put all his men at her disposal and Caroline got a great story. Indeed, it was so good that *Life* published it with her by-line, gave her a raise, and officially promoted her to the position of aviation editor.

Other interesting assignments followed. A story on aerial war photography involved all the latest developments in army methods of taking aerial war photos. A story on precision bombing was the toughest assignment Caroline ever had; it took six months of hard work to finish up this story. Another piece was about girl pilots at Sweetwater.

In the course of her assignments for *Life* Caroline has done a great deal of traveling around the country and has been at the controls of every type of army bomber and many other military planes.

"You know," she says, "all that cross-country flying I did on my own before joining *Life* has helped a lot on these assignments. *Life* is cosmopolitan and I find that a knowledge not only of the various parts of the country, but also of the people in each section, is valuable background for my present work. More than anything else on this job, you have to like people and be able to meet them and talk to them in their own language."

In September, 1944, just preceding the memorable trip to Greenland, Caroline went on a trip with Margaret Bourke-White, foremost woman photographer of this country, who has covered the world's war fronts with her camera. They covered twelve hundred miles in ten days in a T.W.A. Lockheed Electra for a special issue of *Life,* called "A Letter to the GI's." Their purpose was to show how America looked from the air at that moment.

Every corner of the United States was included in the trip—Washington, D.C., to Dayton; Wichita to Tulsa, then to Albuquerque; Phoenix to Los Angeles to Portland, Oregon; Chicago to New York. Margaret Bourke-White took seven hundred pictures on the trip and Caroline's job was to supply the necessary research information and to organize their flight plan and the final sequence of pictures to accompany the story.

"That's what makes my job so fascinating!" Caroline

says. "No two assignments are anything alike. I've always been interested in all sorts of things and I find here that some time or other I use every scrap of knowledge I've ever gathered. I've also found that you need a lot of stamina for this type of job—the hours are uncertain and a lot of travel is necessary. I often make trips on half a day's notice—that request to 'go to Texas tonight' on the *Suzy Q* job was far from exceptional."

But even when tired, Caroline thinks her job at *Life* is a happy one for her. "Some people like free-lance writing for aviation magazines and other publications," she says. "I have done a little of it myself. But I do better with the discipline of a deadline that has to be met. Then, of course, representing *Life* is like having an 'open sesame' for collecting news and learning more about aviation anywhere."

Caroline has found her work the means of discovering new and fascinating aspects of aviation, the people in it, new developments, and the physical and economic problems of the industry, "things I never had any conception of before, when piloting was my chief connection.

"I think young women have a promising future in aviation writing, in fact, in journalism of all kinds. Right now my alma mater is conducting a survey of jobs that are particularly well suited to women in journalism and other fields. These findings seem to point particularly to many new opportunities in the future for girls now in high school and college, jobs in which they have a natural advantage over men, such as home economics and fashion writing, where the male competition is either very slight or nonexistent. There will be a variety of writing, advertising, and editorial jobs for girls in aviation in the future."

Now that the war is over, Caroline hopes to do more personal flying. She has taken only two personal trips since working for *Life*, flights to Mexico in the summers of 1944 and 1945 with another *Life* staff member.

"Some day," Caroline adds, "along with a million other girls, I hope to marry and settle down to raise 'little flyers,' but until that time I expect to stay with *Life* and help the world fly by!"

ETHEL COLWELL

MORE than half a million women held jobs in the aircraft industry by the end of the Second World War. Today, of course, the majority have left aircraft factory benches to return to their own kitchens, or to the same typewriter they pounded before the war. Women no longer comprise nearly half the employees in some of our large aircraft plants. "Rosie the Riveter" has had her day, but she did fine work when she was desperately needed! By the end of the war, women were doing 60 per cent of the many steps necessary in building an airplane.

The opening wedge has been inserted. There will always be a place for women in the aircraft industry. The trained engineer or draftsman particularly is firmly entrenched. And it is these more highly trained women especially who will serve the aircraft companies and airlines in the future.

In the beginning it was quite a job to help thousands of women, who had never seen a monkey wrench or riveting machine before, settle happily into their jobs in industry. The aircraft manufacturers said it couldn't be done, but women personnel workers knew it could.

In Canada, the task was given to Ethel Colwell, one of Canada's top-ranking women executives whose long experience in dealing with problems of organization made her just the person for the job. She pioneered the first schools for training Canadian women personnel directors. They, in turn, went back to their respective aircraft plants with new knowledge to help them keep women employees safe and happy on the assembly line. Ethel's boundless enthusiasm and imagination could get a job done when others could see only a blank wall. The results of her fine work have become a part of Canada's aircraft industry history.

Ethel was born in Lancashire, England, where as a child she went to St. Swithin's Ladies Seminary. "I learned to knit, sew a fine seam, cook, dance, play the piano and sing a little (none of which jelled on me very well)," she says; "so when we moved to Canada, it was difficult to fit my English education into the Canadian university pattern. While everybody was wondering just what school I should be put into, I decided to take a business course. At the end of six months, having learned to read the 'pot hooks,' I got a job with the Bell Telephone Company as a stenographer. I was then about seventeen."

After Ethel had been with Bell a few months, her boss called her into his office one day and told her that since he had a fatherly interest in her (having daughters about Ethel's age), he felt she should know that he didn't think she'd ever make a good stenographer. "I can still see the letter on his desk with my many typing errors carefully 'blue penciled,'" Ethel adds. "And anyway, I had just about reached the same conclusion. I was no stenographer, I knew that—but I did want to stay with the company."

The Bell Company was having a mild depression at

this time, so employees were urged to try and get more people to have telephones installed, and to change to private lines where they had two-party ones, and add extensions. Ethel had some very definite ideas as to how sales could be increased. So, when by a lucky chance she was seated next to the vice-president in charge of sales at a company "pep-up banquet," she fired a series of questions at him in rapid staccato:

"Why don't we start selling the minute people come to the counter for a new telephone? Why do we let them just take the cheapest sort of service they can get? How do we know that people are using long distance as much as they can afford?"

"Thinking it over many years later," Ethel says, "I still don't know whether it was the sheer audacity of a teen-aged new-comer bringing forward these suggestions to an old established organization, or just that this very kindly vice-president remembered that he had started his own career digging postholes—but he decided to give me a chance. Very quickly I was given a telephone and told to go ahead and see what I could do.

"It turned out very well. In fact, so well, that the company decided to set up similar small 'sell by telephone' departments in all its major offices and I was sent from office to office to train other girls in this type of work.

"Among other things, for training purposes we established a system of listening by microphone to actual sales conversations. A stenographer at the other end of the mike took notes, and later these cases were reviewed and used to train future salesgirls. One day I was on duty when a new subscriber came in and ordered a two-party-line wall telephone. With an ease that amazed me, I sold him instead an individual service hand phone, and an extension. Everyone complimented me and the case history was held up as an example of how such selling should be done. Imagine my chagrin when several days later the irate customer telephoned me to find out where the heck his telephone was. In the excitement, I had forgotten to issue the order.

"Some time later the Bell Company started still another project. We did some radio listener interviewing—you know, calling and asking people what program they're listening to and what product is being advertised—similar to work done by Crossley in the United States. I became very much interested, and eventually went to New York to learn more about it.

"This 'listener interviewing work' fascinated me so much I left Bell and went into business for myself. In Canada, we do not jump at ideas so quickly as they do in the United States, so for the first three or four years it was very up-hill work. I had to be educated into market research, but since the whole business was very young, I just grew up along with it. It grew into a sound, worth-while business, called Canadian Facts, Limited, with a head office in Toronto, a sales office in Montreal, and about three hundred full-time or permanent part-time people scattered across the entire country."

At the start of the war, Canada was in exactly the same situation that the United States was in later. There were very few people who knew much about building airplanes, only a few had been built each year. Most of the plants were small and poorly equipped and had never employed women. Out of this chaos, Canada had to quickly build up a great many efficient aircraft plants all across the country.

The aircraft industry in Canada was fortunately placed in charge of a man of action! When several of the plants seemed to be in more than usual difficulties, he decided to ask the employees what their ideas were. So Ethel's firm was commissioned to do what is known as an "employee-attitude study," asking a cross section of employees specific questions about their jobs.

"The day after I presented that report at Ottawa, I was offered a war job," Ethel continued. "I was to be director of women for some thirty-odd aircraft plants throughout Canada—with about 50,000 women employees in all. The duties outlined included designing safety wearing apparel for the women and aptitude testing to find out which job each particular woman was best fitted for. My biggest job was to give a training course for women personnel supervisors, conducting classes in personnel relations for individual plants in five different Canadian cities.

"I wrote this personnel course after quite a bit of research, part of which was done in the United States. In the States they were groping in the dark, just as we were, and wrestling with the same problems caused by the entry of women into war plants. Aircraft industries there were trying to set up a system similar to the one we were working on in Canada, and their thinking ran along the same lines as ours.

"One of the most interesting and encouraging things that happened to me while I was in the United States was an invitation from the Navy aircraft personnel in Washington asking me to bring my course down there and tell them about it. As I landed at the beautiful Washington airport, a lieutenant commander and two aides, all dressed in their best uniforms, stepped up, saluted, and said: 'Very happy to have you aboard.' I was very much impressed!

"The cooperation between Canada and the United States on this work was certainly remarkable. I have the very highest regard for everyone in the United States with whom I worked."

Ethel Colwell returned to Canada to begin classes throughout the dominion for women plant supervisors. No one could have been found better by nature, background, and experience to do such a job. Her personality and approach were dynamic, her methods sound— and through all the training her contagious enthusiasm stimulated every woman in the group. She was at her best when faced with a tough job, as organizing this women's group promised to be. The larger the difficulty, the brighter the gleam in her eye, for Ethel Colwell has a breadth of vision far beyond that of the usual organizer. She could visualize the real needs of women workers in Canada's aircraft industry and so could do something about it.

Ethel's first class of fifteen students in Ontario ranged from girls in their twenties to gray-haired matrons. They formed an interesting cross section of the women working in Ontario aircraft plants. One student was a widow with a son in the Royal Canadian Engineers in England, another had played a harp at concerts throughout North America before she decided to help Canada build planes, and still another was a large, stout, redhead who looked like anything but what she was—a gifted sculptress.

"I don't think I've ever enjoyed anything more than I did giving this course," Ethel says. "I don't know why that is exactly, except that the women were so interesting and it was a definite, concrete, worth-while job—something you could see through from beginning to end in six months and not have any loose ends hanging around afterward."

Under Ethel's direction the aircraft industry prepared an attractive booklet called *Women Safe at Work*, which told employees about the many services offered to them by the company. It dealt with health, diet, safety, care of eyes, what to wear, and the like. For instance, first aid and hospital services were provided to safeguard the health of employees. The company had found that it paid to do so, for in one year alone industrial accidents had resulted in an estimated loss of 5 million work days. This is the equivalent of a plant employing 20,000 workers standing idle for an entire year. In terms of thousands of planes stalled along the production lines, these figures sobered a nation determined to do its utmost.

The booklet also contained safety headlines: "Before starting a new job, be sure that you understand the instructions given by your foreman. Never take chances. Try to develop a calm and quiet way of working to promote safety. According to records, fingers, feet, and eyes are most often the victims of accidents. Save yours from painful injury by wearing protective clothes, goggles, and shoes. Lift and carry correctly. If there is any possibility of eye injury on the job that you are doing, be sure to wear safety goggles."

Extensive surveys were made regarding clothing for

workers. The great influx of women war workers called for something better than the old conventional type of overalls. Plants were greatly concerned about the type of slacks and miscellany of female work clothing being worn, chiefly because much of it was impractical and dangerous. A variety of garments for women were created and shown by models at meetings of industry executives in the plants. Employees were asked for their opinions. As a result, smarter appearing, more practical work outfits were developed, many of which were soon in great demand by other industries.

Ethel Colwell packed every minute of the five eight-hour days of the course with information imparted for the most part by lectures and films. The films dealt with specific jobs being done by women in war plants and were intended to give the "house mothers" a wider understanding of the problems faced by women who did these jobs.

She stressed safety rules and made it clear that these rules were only common sense and formulated for the worker's own protection. She spoke of the many benefits offered by the company, such as group insurance, health insurance, visiting-nurse service, in-service training by which a worker may prepare herself for a better position, and nonprofit cafeterias and child-care centers.

The fifteen "house mothers," trained to keep Ontario girl war workers happy, graduated from their unique course at Toronto Central Technical School and returned to their own plants with new knowledge. The course was the first of its kind, but others were planned—the hope being that a "house mother" could be provided for every two hundred women in Canada's aircraft plants.

With thousands of women employees pouring into aircraft plants, naturally there were many problems of adjustment. Foremen and executives could not take care of all the employees' personal problems. An urgent need arose for women personnel supervisors in the fast-growing aircraft industry. Some solution had to be found if the industry was to put forth its best effort, for an unhappy employee could not do an efficient job. Someone had to help women employees with their personal problems.

Ethel Colwell's trained personnel counsellors were the answer. They did everything to help keep the employees happy on the job, from finding a living place, to making medical and dental appointments when necessary, and even finding someone to take care of the children while the mother was at work. The majority of these counselors had educational or social-service backgrounds and they were friendly, tactful women who took a real interest in the welfare of the employees. Each one also had enough practical working experience so that she could offer the employees workable solutions for their problems.

"These problems were many and varied," Ethel Colwell adds. "A red-eyed mother comes in to say she is quitting because she can't find anyone to get her children's evening meal. The counselor quiets her, arranges to have her shift changed so she can be home to get supper for her children, and another happy employee returns to the assembly line.

"Another girl comes into the counselor's office, angry and defiant. She just can't work with the foreman in her department who doesn't like women workers and 'rides' her all the time, she says. A talk with the foreman and then again with the girl results in her shift to another department and all is serene.

"Strangely enough one of the most frequent difficulties was getting a girl to take a promotion she had earned. She seemed to resent it sometimes as if it meant she weren't doing her original job well, or else she liked the girls in the first department and was happy there. The personnel counselor really had a hard job promoting a girl sometimes."

Employees on every shift were provided with lunchtime entertainment because it had been discovered that some sort of diversion at lunch time spurred production as much as 11 per cent. Lunchtime fun broke the monotony of the job, aided digestion, and put the worker in a happy frame of mind.

Complicated jobs done by highly trained mechanics before the war were broken down into a number of simple operations which could be learned quickly and easily by women workers. Platforms were built so that smaller women could have their work at a comfortable height. Jigs, in which parts were placed for assembly, were built lower to accommodate women workers. Hand and foot pedals on machinery were reset.

Women were found to be particularly good as aircraft inspectors because they were so conscientious about their work. They were more careful of tools and materials, too, and did a job as they are told without taking dangerous short cuts.

They received the same salary as men for the same work. In certain types of work which required fine handwork, patience, and a delicate touch, women did a better job than men. And they never seemed to mind doing the same job over and over.

"Most of the jobs held by women," Ethel adds, "were not skilled operations, but a few girls did show outstanding ability in mechanical work. I remember one girl in Toronto who became an expert electrician while at the plant. She could take a whole generator apart and put it together again quickly and skillfully.

"Another girl at a plant in Vancouver was an expert in the machine shop. For instance, she could sharpen a file better than any man in the plant. These two girls looked enough alike to be sisters, which interested me so much that I told each about the other. Last time I heard the two girls had gotten together and intended opening their own garage.

"What the future of women in aircraft will be is anybody's guess at this point," Ethel Colwell says. "If the 'flivver' type of airplane becomes widely used, as we expect it will, many war plants can be utilized and the women who were trained to do small operations in war plants will be able to do similar work when the plant converts to other types of aircraft. But, in Canada at least, most of the plants will be used for manufacturing other commodities. There were really only a very few women who did advanced types of operations. The majority were trained for one particular operation in a matter of weeks or days and they can learn similar operations in the manufacture of automobiles or vacuum cleaners if they wish.

"Where they can do the operation better than men and where it seems more suitable to use women, aircraft manufacturing jobs will always be open to them. You must remember that much of what was published about women in war industries was publicity to get more women into aircraft plants where they were terribly needed.

"In talking to these girls who worked in aircraft plants during the war (I did a small survey on the subject about two years ago), I found that many intended to go back to their original occupations when the extremely high salaries were no longer offered and the excitement of working in a war industry was over.

"I think I'd sum it all up by saying I don't think that there is a big new career in aircraft for women, but that definitely some of the women who want to work in plants will find jobs there."

VALENTINA GRIZODUBOVA

SOVIET RUSSIA is the only country in the world which has allowed its women to become combat pilots. In the Second World War many of the several hundred women fighter and bomber pilots in the Red Air Force became combat aces. At the beginning of the war, the Russian government officially frowned upon women in combat flying, but as German oppression increased, many were allowed to join in the air fight against the Nazis.

No matter how we feel as a nation about women as combat pilots, much as we do not want this in America, we must admire the skill and courage of these Russian women fighters. Women pilots all over the world share the reflected glory of their fine record. Perhaps if we had seen our parents murdered and our homes destroyed by Nazi invaders, we American women would also find it an easy transition from ferry pilot to bomber pilot.

The Soviet Union is more advanced in general airmindedness than any other Allied country. Long before the outbreak of war she realized the value of gliders as preflight training to build a great military air reserve. All her physically fit young people were encouraged to take glider training, as a screening process, to eliminate the unfit and leave a vast pool of material for future combat pilots. The Soviet government was saved tremendous expense therefore in training fighter pilots because potential wash-outs were eliminated before entering any advanced training program.

At the beginning of the war, Russia had one million glider pilots ready for combat training. They had all we had, and more, in aviation equipment and training, too, for the Russian people were so indoctrinated in air-mindedness since early childhood that they literally thought in terms of a third dimension.

The most outstanding Russian woman combat pilot is Colonel Valentina Grizodubova. She is one of a very few who have received the high award of "Hero of the Soviet Union," similar to the Medal of Honor in the United States. Thirty years ago when Valentina was born, the airplane was in its infancy, and the two grew up together. Her biography parallels the development of aviation in the Soviet Union.

Valentina's mother was a seamstress, her father a designer and inventor. His life was a struggle, like that of so many inventors, and his family often knew what the wolf at the door looked like. Mr. Grizodubova had a real genius for aircraft construction and as early as 1908 built a primitive flying machine, similar to the first practical plane designed and flown in the United States.

Like the Wright Brothers, Mr. Grizodubova built this plane at his own expense, with the help of a few interested fellow workers. His early ideas were turned down by the government, but he persevered and eventually some measure of fame and fortune came his way.

Having no son, Valentina's father saw nothing unusual in having his daughter share these initial flights with him. At Kharkov, Mr. Grizodubova and his three-year-old daughter were allowed by the town authorities to make flights together, if they promised "not to trample the grass or frighten the horses," reflecting the attitude of the day toward such "crazy goings-on." They went to many glider meets and spent long afternoons soaring upward on the favorable currents over the mountain slopes.

Both were enthusiastic travelers. Geography was Valentina's favorite subject at school, and at home she and her father read together all the stories of travel they could find. Anything from a trip to Spain to fantastic dreams of a visit to the moon interested them. When Valentina's father went on one of his frequent business trips, he wrote vivid descriptions of his travels in letters to his small daughter. It was really these letters which stimulated Valentina's thinking about the far-eastern flight which later made her famous.

As she grew older, her desire to learn to fly increased. She was no longer satisfied to be a passenger on flights with her father; she wanted to fly on her own. So, at eighteen, Valentina enrolled in the Kharkov Technological Institute, realizing that a fundamental knowledge of science and mechanics is helpful to any pilot. While she was a student at Kharkov, she met Sergo Ordjoinkidge, Stalin's right-hand man. He was very much impressed by her knowledge and enthusiasm. This was the chance she had been waiting for, and she poured her flying ambitions into his sympathetic ears.

A year later this contact bore fruit. Valentina was admitted to one of the finest flying schools in Russia. In the next few years she studied at several schools, gaining as many different approaches to aviation as she could. Finally, she ended up at the Osoarviakhim, a large national air school, which before the war had about 58,000 members.

Soon Valentina had her pilot's license from this school, but she still didn't know nearly enough about aviation to satisfy herself. So she stayed on there for an advanced course, and eventually became a flight instructor for the Osoarviakhim. The next year when the school held its annual aerial contest, in which members competed for flying honors, Valentina walked off with several championships.

Soon Valentina was looking for a way to widen the scope of her flying activities. She joined the Maxim Gorky Escadrille (named after the famous Russian statesman and writer) and flew around the country spreading educational pamphlets about agriculture, industry, and science to remote parts of the Soviet Union. These trips made the geography she had studied come alive to her as she flew from town to town in her flying laboratory transport plane.

As the first woman to be accepted by the Escadrille, Valentina's work opened up a whole new life to her. She traveled from one village to another giving lectures and showing films to the local people, who for the most part had no contact with, and very small knowledge of, the outside world. It was the first time most of them had seen an airplane, so a woman pilot was no more astonishing to them than the fact of flight itself. Valentina was an enthusiastic, inspiring speaker, and her audience listened eagerly to everything she told them about the government, about the world outside their small village, and about aviation.

Later it was discovered that hundreds of girls from these villages where Valentina had talked were fired with a desire to fly, eventually becoming combat pilots for Russia. Sometimes as many as 130,000 people gathered at one of the Escadrille meets to hear her and got stiff necks watching the spectacular parachute jumping and stunt flying that was a part of the program.

There was an era in aviation, not only in Russia but in every country in which aviation was coming of age, when record breaking flights were rampant. Men and women flew oceans, attempted nonstop speed flights for great distances, visited the North Pole or tried endurance flights with refueling in midair. The object of these spectacular performances was to stimulate public interest in aviation and to prove the powers of this "newfangled contraption"—the airplane. For women particularly this was about the only way they could make a real contribution to aviation at the time.

Naturally Valentina, as Russia's foremost woman flyer, set out to break a few records. And she did a good job of it! In one week she captured three world records for women. She flew a single-seater plane over a triangular course of 100 kilometers to establish a new record of 220 k.p.h. over the American record of 198 k.p.h. Two days later she beat another American record in a two-seater, with a woman mechanic aboard, with 200 k.p.h. over a former record of 127 k.p.h. That same day she established a third world record in a hydroplane of 195 k.p.h. over the previous record of 107 k.p.h.

The Russian people, grateful for the honor she had brought to their country, elected her as deputy to the Supreme Soviet, the legislative body of the Soviet

Union. This "Congress" is made up of outstanding people from every field, whether agriculture, aviation, or literature. It is not an organization of politicians, but of experts who have become distinguished in their own particular fields.

Before long Valentina and Marina Raskova, another woman pilot, were talking about a great nonstop flight from Russia to the Far East. They made their plans carefully and soon were making trial flights in an advanced model, low-winged, twin-engined transport, which had an air-cooled engine and separate instrument boards for pilot and copilot. A third woman, Pauline Ossipenko, joined them and the three worked hard to get ready for the big flight.

Soon they were all set to go, waiting only for Stalin's verdict as to whether they could make such a flight in the name of the Soviet government. He had displayed considerable interest in their original plans and had been watching all preparations carefully. Finally, one day near the end of their trial flights, the three women received a telephone call from Stalin's headquarters asking them to report immediately. Half an hour later a car arrived at the airport to take them to the Kremlin, the seat of the government, and in the car was the commander-in-chief of the Red Air Force.

Valentina tells of her meeting with the head of her government much as an American girl might record a visit to the White House. "On our arrival we were conducted immediately into Comrade Stalin's headquarters. I was very excited. I had seen him several times before from a distance during public appearances at state affairs, but I had never before spoken to him personally. As we knocked on the door, a deep voice said 'Come in,' and as we did so, Comrade Stalin rose and walked toward us with an outstretched hand. His warm smile and cordial manner soon put us at ease."

Molotov was present at this meeting, too, and several other high officials of the Soviet government. The group sat for hours discussing the forthcoming trip.

Stalin set his seal of approval upon the project, and a few weeks later the three girls started on an adventure which took them through storms, over miles of mountains and forests, from Moscow to the Soviet Far East. They established a world record of 6,450 kilometers (about 4,000 miles) for a long-distance flight. This was the first of many long-distance flights the three made together. Today Valentina is the only one of the trio still alive; the other two women were killed in action over Germany.

Valentina captured a few more international altitude records, and then settled down to earth for a while to be married and have a son, and to become chairman of the Women's Anti-Fascist Committee of Moscow.

But before long the Nazis invaded Russia, and Valentina, along with many other Russian women pilots, volunteered their services to the government. For a time women were limited to essential flying jobs behind the front lines, ferrying medical supplies, doctors and nurses, and wounded soldiers back and forth from front lines to hospitals. This type of work was a very natural outgrowth of the part Russian women had played in aviation before the war.

Participation of women in the science and mechanics of aviation was nothing new in that country. From the very beginning, when Russia first decided that its citizens should become familiar with aircraft and parachute jumping, air-minded young women swelled the membership of the Osoarviakhim for national defense. They particularly excelled at parachute jumping, making record jumps of nearly 27,000 feet without oxygen masks.

The number of women pilots grew as civilian aviation grew, until passengers, cargo, and even mail were being transported over the enormous expanse of Russia by women pilots. It was difficult terrain for flying, but even snow-capped mountains and long sea-plane flights over broad Russian waters didn't faze them. When you consider the enormous size and scattered population of Russia, you realize why aviation gained ground so rapidly in that country.

Although her 8½ million square miles of land encompass one-sixth of the land surface of the world, the Soviet Union is thinly populated proportionately, having only about one-fourteenth of the earth's people. Less than one-tenth of the Russian people live in towns; most of them are farmers, fishermen, trappers, and miners in a country which includes every type of climate and terrain. Small wonder then that a foresighted government was quick to recognize the utility of the airplane in bringing scattered peoples closer together.

Even before the war, planes were used extensively to transport fresh fish from the north to central regions of the U.S.S.R., fruits from distant places without spoiling, and furs, sulphur, and gold to large cities in record time. Considerable crop dusting was done by plane in the farmlands, and aero-chemical battles were fought with malaria mosquitoes. Women were eligible for any of these jobs there on an equal basis with men.

Before the war they were way ahead of us in this re-
spect. Since their value to civilian aviation had already
been acknowledged, no objections were raised, when
war came, and women went on to do other types of
flying.

As Valentina said: "There are no special female professions in our country—no 'women's business.' There
is no sphere, no branch of industry, culture, or life in
general where women are not a mighty force. They
have attained honor in science, art, and technology—
in every sphere of human activity."

A women's fighter unit flew with brilliance at the
battle of Stalingrad. There a night bomber outfit
staffed entirely by women under the command of a
woman flyer bombed enemy railroad junctions, supply
trains, and ammunition dumps so successfully that the
group was given the honorary title of Grand Air Unit,
and each of the members received a distinguished
service medal.

The fighter pilot unit working with this bomber
outfit was based forty to sixty kilometers behind the
front lines. On these springboard landing fields the
pilots who were on duty stayed in the cockpits of their
planes. They waited there for word of any enemy
planes sighted. The take-off signal was given by the
wireless operator who received the message from the
front line. By firing a Very pistol, the officer in charge
indicated the areas where enemy planes were to be
intercepted. Additional information as to the altitude
and number of the enemy was transmitted to each
plane by wireless after they took off.

As soon as the first line of planes had taken off, a
second line of planes moved up into the first position.

The Soviet fighters were more active than the Germans
and accepted battle under any conditions, though
sometimes almost hopelessly outnumbered. Their fierce
fighting and daring maneuvers compensated for the
uneven balance, and the enemy's superior numbers
dispersed into disorderly retreat.

This was only one of many air battles and bombing
raids participated in by an ever increasing number of
women as the war progressed. As soon as the government's prejudice against women combat pilots lessened
its grip even a little, practically every woman pilot in
Russia was applying for combat service in preference
to safer ways of helping to win the war. But as is usually the case, there were enough left who could not
qualify for combat service to take care of auxiliary flying duties.

Teamwork was the all-important thing, the watch-
word for men and women pilots alike. After an initial
reluctance which was quite natural, the men worked
willingly as equals with women pilots. They did not
mind when the plane's commanding officer was a
woman and they had to take orders from her. Soviet
bomber crews were soon very proud of their feminine
plane mates, and as Valentina says: "The men are embarrassed now to remember that in the early days we
were not nearly so welcome."

Girls who before the war had flown only in their
spare time at air clubs were now flying around the
clock in night bombing raids on German cities and in
daytime encounters with the Luftwaffe. Some of them
had downed as many as twenty planes by the end of
the European war.

Even French fighter pilots who were assigned to

escort Russian women bomber pilots to their missions behind Nazi lines had nothing but praise for their ability. "These girls are among the best bomber pilots in Russia," said the chief of the Normandy unit of De-Gaulle's fighters on the Soviet front.

This desire of Russian women to bomb German cities was born of a deep-seated hatred of the enemy that in our smug safety we may too easily condemn. Valentina makes the attitude of one woman pilot a little easier to understand:

"The Germans killed her mother, father, and one of her children—only her younger son survived. Her hatred for our enemies was as great as her tenderness for her surviving child. None of her bombs missed their aim."

She said of another, whose entire family had been wiped out by Nazi invaders: "In her dark eyes lay the shadow of profound grief, but her handshake was as firm as a mans. To avenge the dead, to assure a better future for the living—that is why we Russian women went up to battle the Nazi foe."

These women are not warlike Amazons. They had no love of killing for its own sake—they did what they felt they had to do. If you could have seen them sitting around the airdrome between flights, doing fancy work and embroidery in the incongruous setting of a war-time airfield, dressed in nondescript flying suits, you would realize that essentially war did not change them. Now that it is over, many a Russian woman who a short time ago flew into combat against Messerschmitts and Focke-Wulfs has returned to her farm, her home, and her children.

HELEN MONTGOMERY

FLIGHT without power is the one branch of aviation most truly a sport. The Second World War proved the glider a valuable military weapon; towed cargo gliders of the future will prove its commercial value, and its scientific contributions to aviation in meteorology and aerodynamics are indisputable. But for all that, motorless flight is still primarily a sport.

We are only now beginning to recognize that gliding is the safest and sanest introduction to flying and to make it no longer the stepchild of aviation.

Helen Montgomery has been the foremost woman glider pilot in the United States for many years. She was one of the first women to get a glider license, and she has soared higher, farther, and longer in a glider than any other woman in this country. During the war she trained many of the army glider pilots who later took part in European air-borne invasions.

The end of the war brought Helen back into the ranks of sportsman glider pilots, for she would be the first one to emphasize that, on the whole, gliding does not offer women a career. During the war a few women glider pilots did earn a living in temporary positions as army instructors, but basically gliding is a sport like golf or tennis. And although, as in other sports, a few glider pilots have turned professional, the majority are interested in gliding just for the joy of the sport. The fascination of motorless flight offers the enthusiast a thrill and a satisfaction that power flying can never offer, as anyone who has done both will tell you.

Helen was born in the city of Fort Wayne, Indiana. The family moved frequently, making her schooling something of a hit-and-miss affair. She attended every type of school from the most rural one-room affair to a large city high school with thousands of students.

"This family wanderlust must have been transmitted to me in some way," Helen says, "because even after we finally did settle down, I was always running away to my grandmother's house. I nearly always got train-sick on these trips but it didn't keep me home. The surprising thing is that I wasn't bothered with motion sickness in an airplane later on. I've never turned green in a plane or glider, although I've done plenty of acrobatics and have flown through a few terrible storms which came up unexpectedly."

Unfortunately there was no money to send Helen to college, although she had graduated from high school at sixteen with high scholastic honors. The market crash came after she had been working in an office for a short time; and, with the depression, her last hope of a college degree flew out the window. A favorite aunt came to the rescue with a little financial help, however; and Helen, after three years of struggle, was graduated from the University of Michigan School of Nursing.

Although it was at best a second choice, this nurse's training proved to be the turning point in Helen's life.

While she was at Michigan, she met and married Law-rence Montgomery, a graduate physicist at the univer-sity, and he introduced her to aviation. They soon moved to Cleveland, home of the National Air Races, and as Helen put it: "As I watched other women per-form in these aerial events, I became very air conscious and made up my mind then and there to get into the exciting and adventurous field of aviation some day, somehow! Friends of ours were learning to fly and they talked about it all the time. Larry was very much interested too, but at the moment, since he was return-ing to college to get his Ph.D., flying seemed too expen-sive a proposition and had to be temporarily shelved. Two years later our patience was rewarded. We moved to Ann Arbor where a glider club had recently been formed and Larry became a member immediately. I, for some reason, remained only an interested spectator and helper for a while."

Before long Helen was taking lessons in an Aeronca, a 36-horsepower, two-cylinder "flying bathtub." So while Larry learned to operate a glider, Helen learned to fly a powerplane. A perfect combination! Eventu-ally the two joined forces and changed places, Helen took up gliding, and Larry got a private pilot's license.

"I'll never know," Helen says, "how it happened that I was entrusted with the club's precious glider for a first flight when I wasn't even a member, but I was allowed to make two flights, each of about thirty sec-onds duration. The next day, to everyone's astonish-ment, especially my own, I made a gliding flight of one hour's duration, earning my "C" license. There I was, the possessor of a soaring license with only three flights in my book—and when I think of the months of struggle some neophytes have to gain this license—I was just lucky!"

There is a definite distinction between gliding and soaring. Gliding is a flight in which no altitude is attained above the point of release. The glider is launched and floats to earth in a few minutes, as a beginner learns to use the controls and get the feel of flying. In soaring, a lighter, more maneuverable type of glider called a sailplane is usually used; and, after release from the winch which launches it into the air, the soaring pilot seeks upward air currents, which he utilizes to gain altitude. Altitudes of almost 30,000 feet—more than five miles straight up—without any power other than the air currents, have been attained by soaring pilots.

The Montgomerys made annual pilgrimages to the national soaring contests at Elmira from 1936 until the beginning of the war. Helen took part in all these contests as a member of the XYZ Soaring Club of Michigan. The Montgomerys with a third enthusiast, had started the organization of this club after their return from Cleveland. All their spare time for many months had been used to drum up members and collect contributions for the work the club was doing. It was a very successful venture, for the club soon had three gliders and a dozen members. In the winter they flew off the ice on Lake St. Clair, and in summer the group attended local meets and prepared for the annual contests at Elmira. It was the most active gliding club in the country at the time.

"We had bought the Aeronca and still used it for cross-country flights, but most of the time it took a back seat for our glider flights, which were much more fun. We were really dyed-in-the-wool enthusiasts by now. One summer we even moved into the two-room structure at our new gliderport. This served as a combination home and hangar so that we could be on the spot all the time."

In 1938 Helen, now the proud possessor of a commercial glider license, hung up an endurance record for women of 7 hours and 28 minutes—almost a full working day spent soaring upward in a glider on air currents. Next she established an altitude record of 4,183 feet and a distance record of 15 miles for American women glider pilots.

Compared with a Russian distance record of 465 miles by a woman glider pilot and an altitude record of 28,400 feet by a German, these are not very remarkable, but in this country they were outstanding records. It is no slur upon Helen's fine work to say that we have been far behind other countries in soaring flights. Our records are very meager compared with Russia's for instance, and American women interested in the sport have been very few indeed.

Helen stunted her "midwest sailplane" at air shows throughout the country. A crowd of twenty thousand gathered in August, 1940, to witness exhibition flying at the annual air show at Pontiac. Helen put her graceful ship through rolls at two thousand feet, and from an altitude of four thousand feet performed twenty consecutive loops on the way down. A series of wingovers topped off what is really a wonderful performance in a sailplane. In fact, Helen won sixth place in the show, the only woman in a group of sixty-three contestants.

The outbreak of war placed government restrictions

on private flying of all kinds, and the XYZ Club became inactive. The three gliders were sold to the government, anxiously searching for such equipment, and
many of the club members became glider instructors
in army contract programs. The Montgomerys accepted positions in the army glider program at Lamesa,
Texas, Larry heading up the ground school, Helen in-
structing glider pilots.

"The civilian contractor who operated the school
had done something quite unprecedented in employing
a woman to instruct glider pilots for the army," Helen
says, "but I guess it was pretty hard to find glider instructors at the time—there were only a handful of
qualified ones in the country."

The students at Lamesa were all volunteers for
glider training, a nice group to work with, and the
work was very interesting to Helen.

"It had its amusing as well as hazardous side," she
continues. "For instance, the students were instructed
to address their instructors as 'Sir' and they had a
hard time choosing between that and a preference for
'Ma'am' in my case. Some of them got quite balled up
and embarrassed when they said 'Sir' by mistake.

"As for hazards, the night flights offered enough
thrills for anyone. Even with the most careful plan-
ning and diligence on the part of the instructor, the
glider frequently got out of range of the airport and
in some tight spots. Students found night flying con-
fusing and many literally didn't know the direction of
'up.' Usually an airplane took off towing several gliders
behind it, attached to each other. When the night
lights occasionally went out on the tow plane or gliders,
there were some awful moments trying to stay in your

proper place in the tow. There was always the possibility that a confused student would pull the release at the wrong time and send you down into unknown, unlighted territory for an emergency landing. This happened quite frequently during daytime flights, but I don't remember that any of our group ever had to make such an emergency landing at night—which was fortunate.

"One of the most hair-raising moments I ever had was as a spectator. I saw two gliders being towed by a power plane crash into a house. There was a thunderous explosion, a flash of fire, and then complete silence—in the darkness of the night. It was a horrible experience, just sitting there in the pitch black, waiting until reports came in that the glider students had made good emergency landings and were unhurt. Even the airplane pilot had been able to walk away from a completely demolished ship."

Occasionally Helen, who now had a commercial pilot's license, would turn the tables, and climb into an airplane to tow other students and instructors upward in gliders for practice flights. She was lucky to have this experience because before long the glider program was discontinued, and Helen had to look for another job.

She applied and was accepted as a flight instructor for the W.A.S.P. at Sweetwater, Texas. "It was a grand opportunity," she says. "There were several phases of training going on at the same time, and I was lucky enough to have not only primary training classes but instrument flight classes as well. I don't think I've ever done more interesting work."

Today Helen is back in the ranks of sportsman glider

pilots, which is where she says she belongs anyway. "Gliding is the best sport in the world but you've got to take it seriously. Girls who take up gliding just for the thrill or for publicity won't get far. It's like any other sport—it takes a lot of time and wholehearted devotion to succeed."

And Helen practices what she preaches, devoting all her spare time to soaring flights and glider club organizations. "I used to play bridge, go boating, swimming in summer, ice skating in winter—but no more. Other sports seem so tame compared with gliding. It is ideal for young people, teaching them team work in operating a winch, assembling a glider, and doing all the other chores that are a necessary part of a glider club's activities. It is a constant challenge too, for the glider pilot is learning all the time. He must continually study meteorology and aerodynamics if he is to improve his skill."

The sport of gliding and soaring is a fascinating one. It is an exhilarating experience to seek out and follow invisible currents of rising air miles above the earth, and to know that such a flight is due entirely to your own initiative, knowledge, and skill. Gliding is a healthful outdoor sport which produces a trim figure and alert mind and contributes to your self-reliance and ingenuity.

But it's not all the joy of flight. Gliding includes endless hours of pushing the ships around the field, keeping time sheets, running the winch, driving the retriever car, assembling and dismantling, patching and repairing gliders, splicing broken tow lines, studying meteorology and other pertinent subjects. It is a sport requiring a lot of time and effort if it is to be successful, but the enthusiast is more than repaid.

Gliding was once considered a crazy hobby; today it is a science of tremendous value in war and peace. The difference between a two-minute flight seventy-five years ago and two hours' sustained flight today is the difference between aeronautical experiment and full-fledged motorless flight. Sailplanes today are safe; accidents are extremely rare because the ships are light and land slowly at a flat angle. There was not a single fatality nor serious injury in ten national soaring meets, with dozens of gliders and hundreds of pilots competing.

Gliding is not a dangerous sport if intelligently approached. One club, for instance, has trained six hundred students without a mishap. The reason for this remarkable record is simple. In gliding you "learn to creep before you walk," you start with the plane being towed by a car along the ground, as you learn to master the controls and keep the wings level. Then you do the same thing at ten feet, then at fifty feet, and then at seventy-five feet you begin to practice turns. So, by the time you are ready for free flight you know how to handle the ship. Some gliders are equipped with dual controls so that instruction can be given, the same as in a powerplane.

Some of the flights which have been made in a glider are astounding—perhaps more so to a powerplane pilot than to a complete novice. One American glider pilot rose on thermals to a height of 17,265 feet at 3,000 feet a minute and glided to a landing eighty-five miles away —all within a period of seventy-five minutes. Imagine a flight like that with no motor to help you!

The best soaring conditions are usually found around large masses of white, puff-ball cumulus clouds. Here a pilot can soar for hours, gliding from one cloud to another as the masses continually break up and re-form. Glider pilots have soared into the heart of a thunder cloud, flying blindly upward at a mile a minute until the plane was a cake of ice. Ships climbing 20,000 feet in five minutes have been torn apart in thunderheads, forcing the pilot to bail out. Thunder-cloud flying is very advanced and the only type of soaring that is really dangerous—it is no sport for beginners!

Soaring combines the best features of skiing and sail-boating. It is not difficult to learn. It is not too expensive if undertaken as a club project, and 90 per cent of glider enthusiasts learn to fly in clubs. Eight hundred dollars will cover the cost of a good glider. Therefore, if a club has ten members, the cost over a four-year period would be $20 per year per person.

Glider pilot training programs for boys and girls have already been started in some of the high schools and about thirty colleges and universities throughout the country. This is the ideal place for many more to develop because high schools in particular could operate a program of combined flight training and glider construction at little additional expense to what it now costs to maintain shop classes in vocational schools.

Gliders could be built out of materials that would have to be purchased anyway for shop work. This is not only an ideal method of teaching aircraft construction and the fundamentals of flight, but these gliders could also then be used for the flight instruction. To-day there is plenty of material for gliders and hundreds of ex-military instructors ready to teach gliding to fledglings.

Helen tells us that several state and N.Y.A. programs were set up before the war for building gliders in the schools. The New York State Department of Education is still very interested and active on a limited scale. It seems certain, therefore, that young people will soon have ample opportunity to begin motorless flight on a sound basis.

The novice starts with slope soaring, taking advantage of the upward surge of air caused by winds blowing against the side of a hill. Later he progresses to "thermal soaring," riding warm currents of air upward. Experienced soaring pilots have crossed the Rocky Mountains on these thermals, landing within a foot of a predetermined mark, to prove glider flight is not aimless but can be controlled. And the very experienced can soar even on cloudless days by riding "dry thermals" which you and I can't see from the ground. Distances up to 233 miles have been flown in a glider on a perfectly clear, cloudless day.

The requirements for glider pilot ratings are not so strict as for powerplane ratings. A student glider pilot must be at least fourteen years old. To obtain a private glider pilot rating he must pass a written examination on air-traffic rules and complete at least 100 gliding flights, demonstrating a certain proficiency.

To obtain a commercial glider pilot rating he must be at least eighteen, pass a written examination, complete at least 250 gliding flights or 200 gliding flights and 5 hours of soaring, at the same time performing more advanced maneuvers. He must also have had at least 1 hour of instruction in recovery from stalls and spins by a certified instructor in an airplane of 1,500 pounds or less.

In addition to these ratings given by the C.A.A., the Soaring Society of America issues a series of gliding and soaring pins and certificates. A Silver C pin is given to a pilot holding a "C" license who has made two or three soaring flights in which the three following requirements have been recorded on a barograph: distance, 32 miles; altitude, 3,280 feet; duration, 5 hours. Altitude and distance must be established in separate flights. Duration may be obtained with either.

The Golden C pin is awarded to the possessor of a Silver C who has made two additional soaring flights in which the following requirements have been recorded on a barograph: distance, 187 miles; altitude, 9,840 feet above point of release.

"There are four important factors in soaring flight," Helen adds, "the air conditions, the glider, the instruments, and the pilot. The pilot's skill is a very important factor and it is this that makes the sport competitive, for a good pilot with an inferior glider can often outfly a less experienced or less capable pilot with a higher performance glider."

Gliding enthusiasts were overjoyed when flight without power was recently given its first real boost in this country. Congress passed a bill allowing airplane student pilots to take as much as 50 per cent of the required flying hours for a private license and up to 25 per cent of the required flight time for a commercial license in a glider.

Anything which promotes gliding promotes the interests of aviation as a whole. There are many reasons why all of us interested in aviation should give the expansion of motorless flight in this country every boost we can.

Fewer airplane accidents would make the headlines if all pilots started on gliders, not only because it is good basic training but also because it is an ideal screening method for eliminating poor flying risks. If one can't successfully learn to manage a glider, he knows it is foolish to go on to a powerplane, and this may save a life.

Motorless flight requires a fine flying technique, a stall-consciousness that even the best powerplane pilot probably never has. The glider pilot must be really "on the ball" every second if he doesn't want to stall out of the climb.

The emphasis placed on simulated forced landings in any flight-training program shows that this is a universal fear for all powerplane pilots. Every landing in a glider is a forced landing and the pilot learns early in the game how to pick out a good field quickly and land in it safely. Even the air-line pilot gains by this knowledge of forced-landing technique and more than one has used thermals to gain altitude in an emergency.

Gliding is the safest, cheapest, and soundest approach to flying. Pilots who learn first to fly in gliders and then in planes make better pilots, for there is a distinct margin of safety available for the pilot who has learned to think of the motor as an accessory.

"At present there is only one national organization working to promote the development of gliding," Helen reminds us. "The Soaring Society of America has done a fine job against tremendous odds. Since it has never had the government subsidies that European countries have given their motorless flight organizations, it has been terribly limited in what it could do."

How much better the worth-while work of the S.S.A. could be carried on if our government gave the financial help other countries give their glider clubs! The British, for instance, supply up to 70 per cent of the operating and equipment costs for any established club. If the S.S.A. had similar help, we could have a national gliding program as fine as the British.

Even with a much smaller subsidy, thousands of glider clubs could be organized which would permit each member to do all the flying he wanted to do for $65 a year. What an air-minded nation we would be then! With such government assistance the S.S.A. could expand its research program with benefit to the entire aviation industry.

And the S.S.A. deserves such help too! Consider all that motorless flight already has contributed to aviation, even with severe handicaps. The development of the glider has increased our knowledge of materials and structures and has even influenced the design of commercial aircraft. In the field of aerodynamics particularly, gliding has provided us with a whole storehouse of scientific data.

Such developments as the "thermal sniffer," which by being acutely sensitive to temperature changes can detect rising currents of warm air, or a miniature vane, which indicates true angle of attack to notify pilot when he is approaching a stall, add to our knowledge and to our safety in flight of all kinds. Out of the main activities of the annual meets at Elmira have come new scientific theories in meteorology and aerodynamics, which have been put to practical tests. Hundreds of contestants bring with them new ideas to be tried out and improved upon, making their gliders and sailplanes regular flying laboratories with meteorographs, accelerometers, two-way 2½-meter radio equipment, and other instruments.

From the ranks of the S.S.A. came the only competent glider pilots, instructors, and designers this country had when war came and such personnel was so badly needed. They readily answered the call, helped to train thousands of other glider pilots, and helped the government to design practical ships.

The war proved the utility of the glider and value of the glider pilot as we all know. With an eye to the possibility of future conflicts, we realize that gliding is an important factor in promoting a "bred in the bone" air-mindedness for young people of this country. It provides the ideal intermediate link, eliminating any teen-age gap, between young model builders and the engineers, pilots, and mechanics who grow into permanent careers in the aviation industry.

"As a sport for girls, gliding is ideal," Helen says. "It requires not only the skill of maneuvering which is required of power flight, but a feel for lift. It is a constant challenge to the pilot, so it should have a special appeal to American girls, who love challenges. Girls are much more welcome at glider fields than at regular airports, the men are always glad to know another enthusiast.

"Gliding and soaring," she continues, "should have tremendous growth now that the war is over. The sport will become a part of national and state programs for the aviation education of youth. And enthusiasts will increase by the thousands because soaring offers such exciting competition."

Interest in gliding is picking up in this country; but, in spite of the undeniable progress made in recent years, the full development of motorless flight in the United States needs some further boosts.

Not only do we need the development of thousands of glider clubs, and a national program of glider training, but we also need annual meets in many parts of the country to replace one large national meet at Elmira.

We need the production of top-notch, easy to build gliders in kit forms such as the cadet glider adapted to American use from a British design. We need factory models, too, to supplement the few army surplus gliders now available.

Most of the single-seaters cost between $800 and $1,000, the two-place gliders about $2,000. These costs are all right for clubs but rather high for individual ownership at present. However these prices will be lowered as sales increase. All the manufacturers are waiting for is demand.

We need to develop inexpensive instruments for gliders too. Regular airplane instruments used in gliders are extremely inaccurate. In fact, ridiculous as it sounds, it is now necessary deliberately to install vibrators in gliders to simulate the lightplane vibration for which the instruments have been designed.

Perhaps more than anything else, we need glider sites, areas from which gliders and sailplanes can be launched without fear of commercial traffic. Hangars where they can be safely stored when not in use will eliminate the time-consuming process of fitting together and disengaging them.

If the future security of our nation lies in its air

power, but if we can't afford to maintain an inactive fleet of thousands of airplanes, gliding is the answer to this problem. It is the easiest way to popularize flying with all young people and to give our nation a backlog of half a million potential combat pilots for training if an emergency arises. And in the meantime we shall be developing the energies and imaginations of our best young people in aviation to make America queen of the skies among all the nations of this world.

PHOEBE OMLIE

A SMALL girl with an earnest face framed by a saucy sailor hat stepped into the Curtiss Field office and announced in a low, matter-of-fact voice: "I'd like to buy an airplane."

The Curtiss salesman's mouth opened and shut several times like a fish gasping for air, but he finally managed to say: "Sit down and we'll talk it over!"

The pertinent facts were soon in his possession . . . Phoebe Fairgrave, seventeen . . . two weeks out of a St. Paul business school . . . had just left a good job with an insurance company because she couldn't stand to be cooped in . . . her grandfather had just left her $4,000 and she wanted to buy an airplane and take lessons . . . when could she start?

This was too much for the salesman. In the 1920's a woman setting foot on an airport, even accompanied by her husband or older brother, was a rare thing, more ridiculous than anything else . . . but to have one calmly walk in alone to buy a plane . . . he called out desperately for the other flyers to come to his rescue.

The salesman explained the situation quickly. One pilot, hoping to get to the root of the matter in a hurry asked: "Miss Fairgrave, have you ever been up in a plane?"

"Oh no," Phoebe answered, "but I want to very much."

The men's faces cleared. Here was a solution to the problem! "I think it can be arranged," the salesman said smoothly and in an aside to the pilot added: "Give this kid the works, Ray. Make her good and sick. Get this flying bug out of her system right now!"

But it didn't work. Phoebe had a wild ride, of course, gritting her teeth and wondering how much longer her stomach would stay where it belonged, but she was game all right. Looking very green at the end of the flight, she emerged from the plane and asked: "When can I start flying lessons?"

"You're too little and much too young!" was the verdict of the pilots. All but one—Capt. Vernon Omlie (a skilled bombing instructor during the first war and then a stunt flyer), stepped up and said: "I'll teach you to fly."

So Phoebe bought a Curtiss Jenny and Vernon taught her to fly.

"What are you going to do once you have a license?" Vernon frequently asked his student between flights. "You'll never be able to earn your living. People in America have no vision now of the tremendous industry aviation will some day become. They think of it in terms of thrills and aerial acrobats. I earn my living by stunting because there aren't any solid opportunities even for a man these days. Without an income how are you going to make out?"

And one day Phoebe answered: "I'm going to do stunts too. I'll learn parachute jumping."

Everyone at the airport was aghast when they heard this, but once again Vernon reluctantly agreed to take her up for her first jumping lesson "if you're crazy enough to try it."

Little did he know as he fastened a parachute on her for a first jumping attempt that the enterprising Miss Fairgrave had marched downtown the day before to the offices of the Fox Moving Picture Company and sold them $3,500 worth of assorted aerial stunts, including wing-walking, parachute jumping, and a few others she had thought up on her way to the office. All she had to do now, of course, was to learn how to do these things. Once again Phoebe had put the cart before the horse.

Vernon hoped she would balk at the last minute and give up this mad idea of parachute jumping once and for all. But no, she jumped. It was quite a procedure in those days. First, she fastened the harness about herself and went aloft. At the proper altitude she left the cockpit, walked out to the end of the wing, attached the harness to the parachute, and then jumped, the weight of her body pulling the parachute from its bag. Once she came down in a lake, once in a tree, but soon she was pinch-hitting for Pearl White in the famous "Perils of Pauline" for Fox movies. She blushes today when she recalls these foolhardy stunts, but in those days there was no other way into aviation for a woman.

Phoebe, Vernon, and Phoebe's brother joined forces to form a flying circus and tour the country. The high light of the show was a parachute jump from fifteen thousand feet by Phoebe, setting a world record for women. She also performed acrobatics on the wing of the plane in midflight and took triple parachute jumps, cutting away one chute and then falling through space until the second opened, and then the same with a third.

Phoebe suggested changing from one plane to another—but not being completely crazy, the three of them decided they'd better practice it first. So they found a long barn and rigged up a trapese bar hanging from the rafters. Phoebe's brother mounted the bar, hung by his knees and extended his hands. Phoebe balanced herself on the back seat of the buggy while Vernon piloted the team of horses. They practiced until Phoebe could come at her brother at a fast trot and still grasp his hands.

Now to try it in the air under much less ideal conditions. The motion-picture people were ready, Vernon piloted one plane, an early air-mail pilot named Short the second, and the camera man was in a third. Phoebe's brother hung from the axle of the upper plane, his hands ready to grasp hers. The two pilots jockeyed their planes into position, and just as they thought everything was all set, a gust of wind hit the lower plane and it climbed rapidly toward the upper one. Phoebe standing on the wing of the lower plane looked up in time to see the propeller of Short's plane almost on top of her. She dropped to her knees, reached under the wing and grabbed a strut, then flipped forward over the edge and shinnied down to the lower wing, out of range of the whirling propeller. The propeller of the upper plane sliced into the aileron of Vernon's plane and almost incapacitated it, but he managed to land safely.

The movie people were still eager for a picture, so the daredevils went up again that same day and did the stunt successfully. But after that they modified it somewhat by having Phoebe grasp a twenty-foot ladder, leaving a more generous margin between the two planes. It was still a spectacular act, and the audience loved it.

Phoebe's only serious accident during this era was a parachute descent into high tension wires which burned her rather badly. She sent a reassuring wire to her mother and then to make doubly sure her mother wouldn't worry, backed up the message by going up as usual and doing her stunts, with one hand and arm bandaged. She sent her mother clippings from the local papers reporting her return to work and then went back to bed for two weeks.

In true story-book fashion, Phoebe and her instructor were married. Soon she and Vernon were looking for a way into serious aviation. And before many months had passed they were running a flying school near Memphis, Tennessee.

Aviation was growing up by now. Air-mail routes with regularly scheduled flights were being organized throughout the country, and passenger travel was encouraged. Even night flying was feasible now with nearly 24,000 miles of air routes equipped with beacons and lights. There was a real demand for good instruction and the Omlie's school prospered. It was hard but very pleasant work for this congenial pair. Their idea was to stress safety before everything else, to prove to the public that the airplane was practical and useful.

Two national disasters occurred about this time to give their aeronautical campaign a boost. Vernon had been backing the formation of a National Guard squadron for the state of Minnesota and getting no-

where. Then a series of very bad forest fires broke out
and he offered to help stop them from the air. On one
flight he spotted and charted eighty-seven fires. He
could tell the firefighters the trends of the fire, as seen
from the air, so they could halt its progress.

Then came the Mississippi flood which Phoebe says
aroused the whole center of the country as to the value
of their mid-South airport. For many days and nights
the two of them did rescue work. They received praise
from all directions for their rescue work and Phoebe
was invited to join the world-renowned organization,
the Ligue Internationale des Aviateurs, as its first
woman member.

The grim work showed an amusing sidelight when
one pilot complained that his ship was logy in the air
and Phoebe asked to have the mail weighed as it was
taken off his plane. The 90 h.p. Waco, built to carry
a maximum of 100 pounds baggage, two passengers,
and a pilot weighing an average of 150 pounds each,
had been carrying 800 pounds of mail!

As a result of their fine work in the flood, political
leaders in Memphis became interested and agreed to
Vernon's plan for a city airport. Their own flying
school was going strong now, and Phoebe felt better
about having turned down a $50-a-day stunting job
with the Law circus. Her days of hanging by her teeth,
knees, and feet from planes were over.

Now for the first time Phoebe entered the field of
competitive flying. Her first undertaking was the National Reliability Air Tour for the Edsel Ford trophy.
The 6,000-mile tour was to cover thirty-two cities in
fifteen different states over some pretty rough country.
Phoebe took off alone in a tiny Monocoupe, the only

woman competitor. In Texas, after landing safely, the small plane was overturned by a sudden gust of wind and the pilot badly shaken. When asked if she were quitting, she said: "Not on your life"; and at Dearborn, the last stop, she stepped from her plane to call to the officials—"Here I am—fooled you, didn't we?" She got more applause than the winner of the trophy.

The next year she made an altitude record for women. In the Dixie Derby of 1930 Phoebe took first prize of $2,000. In 1931 she collected another first in the Handicap Race from Santa Monica to Cleveland, beating fifty-two entrants, including thirty-six men. She won $3,000 and an expensive automobile.

The "Flying Omlies" were a great team, widely acclaimed all over the country, always in aviation projects together, so it was something of a shock to the public when the U.S. government offered Phoebe an aviation job. Acceptance meant that the Omlies would be apart a great deal, but on the other hand, this was something both had wanted for a long time—government participation in aviation.

So off Phoebe went to Washington to inaugurate an air-marking campaign to mark all the important cities. The work fascinated her because it drew on her entire knowledge, skill, and experience.

That year Phoebe was chosen by Mary Margaret McBride as one of the twelve women contributing most to American life. Interviewed by her, Phoebe said: "Of course I still fly. But I'm out of racing for good. I didn't do it for fun ever, and I enjoy my present work so much more. It's a great satisfaction to serve an administration which is really interested in the future of aviation."

Her courage had been tested many times, but never so much as one August night in 1936. Vernon called long distance early in the evening to say: "I'll be up early next week, darling." Later that night, an airliner crashed just outside St. Louis, killing the two pilots and six passengers. One passenger was the distinguished Captain Omlie.

Characteristically, Phoebe continued on in aviation. She resigned her position with the government in order to continue the work her husband had established in Tennessee. Back in Memphis Phoebe accomplished one of the aids to aviation of which she is proudest, and with just reason, because it is intensely practical.

"Hangar flying" one day at a Memphis hotel, she and a political friend discussed the seven-cents-a-gallon state gasoline tax paid by flyers from which they received no visible benefits. They laid plans for diverting part of the tax to the interests of aviation. Both of them realized what a slim chance they had of getting the whole $200,000 in a lump sum. So they set to work and broke it down into ninety-five counties, divided this by the number of towns in the county, and divided it again by the twenty-three different items over which the tax money was spread. This meant that a very small sum went to any one town school board, health department, or road department. Now they could say to a school board, for instance: "You only get $3.25 a year out of this $200,000 which flyers pay in. Would you be willing to spare that much to help Tennessee youngsters get a good training in aviation?"

When it was put that way no one objected, of course. The bill went through the 1937 legislature easily and started a state-wide aviation program which many states have envied and some have copied. This bill made Tennessee the first state to make public funds available for training pilots.

Half of the money was turned over to airports for improvements and the remainder was used to finance ground-school training in the public schools, with seventy-five flying scholarships given in competitive exams. This was years before the government C.P.T. program was organized along similar lines.

In February, 1941, Phoebe was appointed Senior Private Flying Specialist of the C.A.A. and assigned to another practical job, for which her long experience as manager of the airport in Memphis made her well qualified. She started a training program for aircraft and airport service workers. Most of the young men running and servicing airplanes had been drafted, so Phoebe established training classes throughout the country for older men. By the end of the year she had classes started in forty-six states. Seventy per cent of those trained obtained jobs, one of the best placement records ever made in this type of program.

In the fall of 1942, realizing the desperate need for instructors, Phoebe proposed a plan for training women as primary flight instructors. The C.A.A. officials said it was impossible for them to do anything under existing circumstances. So Phoebe took her plan to Tennessee, which she calls her "home state," even though she was born in Minnesota and her mother now lives in Iowa.

The Tennessee Bureau of Aeronautics opened a research school to train ten hand-picked women flyers as instructors.

Phoebe was lent to Tennessee by the C.A.A. to su-

pervise this program. Said Inspector Stanton of the
C.A.A.: "Since women have always excelled in instruct-
ing and have done most of the teaching of our nation,
this should be their natural function in aviation. We
need at least 5,000 women instructors to train 200,000
pilots a year."

Phoebe was very glad to do the job because, as she
said then: "We need a new appraisal of women in war,
particularly in aviation. The whole program of women
in war work always gets distorted by excess publicity,
till you can't see the job for the uniform."

She promised the girls who entered the program that
there would be no glamour attached. "Naturally the
dashing uniformed pilot of the warplane is going to
get more attention than her flight instructor sister—but
women are finding their natural place as instructors."

These girls had to have private licenses and at least
120 hours. The bureau promised them 62 hours of
flying, 216 hours of ground school, 162 hours of flight-
instructor's ground school, and maintenance.

They were housed in an old Tennessee mansion.
Blankets were just not available until Phoebe heard
there were some extra ones at the local penitentiary.
"Let's grab them quickly," she said, "before a crime
wave breaks out!"

Each girl was to be qualified for a ground instructor's
rating in meteorology, aircraft structure, aircraft engines, aerial navigation, and civil air regulations when
she finished the course. They would be able to train
forty pilots a year and give ground school to hundreds.

Out of a thousand applicants, fifteen girls were
chosen for further examination. Psychologists asked
them, "How do you bake a cake?" and check pilots de-

manded: "Do a two-turn spin to the right." Six survived the ordeal, and four more later qualified from
out-of-state.

The first day that the girls reported for their new assignment, they found their director on her hands and
knees scrubbing the last of the floors in the house
where they were to live. She grinned: "See what I
mean, girls, there's no glamour in this business."

The instructor trainees began at 6:45 in the morning, with calisthenics, classes, and recreation scheduled
until 10 P.M., when lights were out. It was a very intensive program; and, to make it harder, at one point
a flood completely submerged the airport. When this
occurred, the resourceful Phoebe merely added a few
subjects to the ground school course for indoor study,
rented a tractor to ferry necessary supplies across the
low ground, and continued with the program.

Based on their success, the Tennessee Bureau of
Aeronautics urged nation-wide instruction programs
for women. The demand for the graduates' services
from school boards and flight instruction contractors
throughout the South was tremendous. One Florida
contractor offered jobs to the whole class.

All this was a direct result of the tax bill Phoebe had
had introduced into the Tennessee legislature years
before.

Now that the war is over, Phoebe is again back in
Washington, doing research on flight-training methods.
Her work includes the installation of photographic
and sound-recording devices in training planes to study
the psychology of the individual learning to fly. Her
particular interest for the future is aeronautical education in the schools. She has already been loaned to

Tennessee by the C.A.A. several times to help that state with its air-education program.

Her wings may not be so new, but Phoebe rates a place in modern aviation on the basis of her flight-instructors school alone. The one real flying opportunity open to women pilots in general today is in the field of flight instruction. Any other flying job is, at the present time at least, probably a one-of-a-kind opportunity that some enterprising woman has made for herself, rather than "a field" which offers jobs for which you can train and qualify.

Phoebe Omlie is one of very few women pilots today who have grown up with aviation from its first record-breaking days to its present status as a great industry. She says: "Judging from my own career, a woman who works hard has an equal chance with men for a job in aviation. We will, of course, not see women captains on airliners any more than we see them on steamships or trains. Women's place in aviation is in private flying."

Phoebe Omlie is living proof that a girl can make a living in aviation, for this grand, unassuming little woman has been doing it for twenty years!

ISABEL EBEL

"IF VARIETY is the spice of life, we sure have plenty of spice in this department! There's no such thing as a typical day. It's a constant race to anticipate questions other members of the organization are going to ask. Any time there's an unusual scientific or technical problem to which no one else can find the answer, we're pretty certain it will end up in here for a solution."

Perched on a stool at her drafting desk in United Air Lines engineering department, elbow-deep in charts and graphs, a keen-eyed, attractive, typically healthy American young woman seeks the answers to innumerable odd questions. Intent on her work, Isabel Ebel's quick mind and accurate fingers are busy figuring calculations on a slide-rule as she studies a blueprint. As the first woman air-line engineer, she is making a real contribution in United's engineering research section to the fine job the air lines are doing these days.

"Would we be able to carry more payload if this airliner were flown at a higher altitude? Could we reduce cargo rates if the plane's average speed were increased? That's the type of question that is handed to us," Isabel continues. "Of course," she adds smiling, "it's all highly theoretical and just on paper—mostly a matter of arithmetic, in fact, but there's a lot of systematic guessing involved that adds to the fun!"

Even in this day of women in overalls, with riveting machines and T-squares in feminine hands a commonplace, a full-fledged woman aeronautical engineer is still exceptional. And you don't become an air-line engineer, especially if you are a woman, by sitting around and waiting for things to happen.

Isabel Ebel had quite a struggle before she reached her present position as aeronautical engineer for United Air Lines, a dual one in fact! First she had to persuade a university to allow her to study for an engineering degree, and then, even after she had it, she had to convince the aeronautical world that engineering ability was not a masculine monopoly. Today her masculine associates readily accept her as a clearsighted engineer, easy to work with, who thinks fast on her feet, and is willing to admit a mistake when she makes one—but it took time.

One wonders, in the face of so much opposition, why Isabel wanted to be an engineer in the first place. Her childhood was in no way unique. She was just a youngster, raised like many others, in the Brooklyn tradition of a public school education liberally mixed with outdoor sports and a tremendous enthusiasm for the Dodgers.

Restless, constantly seeking a new occupation for her keen mind and active body, only one thing set her apart in any way from her fellows—her outstanding ability and consuming interest in mathematics.

In a day when the almost universal idea was: "Oh, she's a girl, of course she's no good at figures," Isabel could do complicated problems in her head in a few minutes that you and I couldn't do with unlimited paper and time at our disposal. At an age when many girls today would be swooning over radio's current crooner, geometry and calculus were fun for her and her recreation as she relaxed in the evening, much as you or I might read a magazine short story.

And why aeronautical engineering specifically? Because Isabel thought she'd find less prejudice in this rather new and enterprising branch of engineering. Once she got into it, she knew that aeronautical engineering was truly the right place for her.

To make this decision was one thing; to get the necessary training quite another. Her civil engineer father told her point blank: "Engineering is no place for a woman!" How many times in the next few years she was to hear that phrase, in different forms, but always with the same discouraging inflection!

Most colleges in the country did not admit women to any courses in engineering, so Isabel did the next best thing. She picked the college nearest home and proceeded to pack as much math as possible into her program.

During her third year at Adelphi college, she investigated Massachusetts Institute of Technology in Cambridge, and found they would not only admit her, but even offer her a half-scholarship because of her fine scholastic record at Adelphi. Next fall she arrived at M.I.T., the only girl studying aeronautical engineering in a student body of three thousand men and thirty girls.

Other girls had started aeronautical engineering at M.I.T. but hadn't finished. It was a stiff course even for one of Isabel's ability and she had to give up the outdoor life she enjoyed to some extent. She was more than willing, however, to give up anything to secure an engineering degree from M.I.T.

The second year she was given a full scholarship; the third year only a half scholarship again, since M.I.T. worked on the theory that if you lasted that long you had enough ability to get outside backing. Isabel's family helped her out.

In 1932 she was given her B.S. degree, plus additional credits for advanced work in aerodynamics, wind-tunnel experiments, and plans on structure and design of airplane models. Isabel Ebel was now the first woman from M.I.T. to receive an aeronautical engineering degree—in fact, the first woman in the United States.

After one year of vain searching for a way into aviation, she decided that perhaps six years of college education (three at Adelphi, three at M.I.T.) and an engineering degree were not enough. She therefore applied for admission to do graduate work at the New York University Guggenheim School of Aeronautics.

The authorities were shocked. No woman had ever dared to enter these sacred portals, and here stood a mere girl, with earnest eyes, calmly seeking admission. "No!" they said, "this we cannot permit!" Why not when she is so well qualified, better in fact than most men applicants? "Why—because she's a woman, of course!"

But that wasn't reason enough for Isabel Ebel. She soon found out that there was absolutely nothing in the university's charter that prohibited women students entering the school of aeronautics. She again attacked the university bigwigs.

She might not have made it, even then, except for a slim, gray-eyed woman, breathing life with every quick, graceful movement, who came to the rescue. With typical determination, Amelia Earhart, by now internationally famous, but never too busy to help a friend, intervened and Isabel was admitted. Later, Miss Ebel plotted Amelia Earhart's course on charts for her when she made her record-breaking transcontinental flight from New York to San Francisco.

They had a great deal in common, these two. Both were pioneers in the cause of women in aviation. Even more than she wanted the training at N.Y.U. for herself, Isabel wanted to make a wedge for other women to study engineering.

One girl among three thousand men students, Isabel certainly never lacked dates.

"Miss Ebel has partially completed some intricate studies of the flying wing design to fulfill requirements for an advanced degree," one newspaper said. "The first candidate of her sex for an A.E. degree at the Guggenheim Foundation of Aeronautics," added another.

"This was really my second contact with the press, though," Isabel says jokingly, "I broke into print the first time in a rather peculiar manner. My mother received a letter from my aunt one day saying she had just received my birth announcement. I was fifteen at the time. The reporters played it up as a human-interest story and no one ever did find out how the announcement had been pigeonholed all that time!"

Once her work at New York University was completed, Isabel decided to return to high school teaching for a while—since there was no alternative anyway at the moment. She had heard that there was an opening to teach mathematics at Brooklyn Technical High School. The principal had frequently said he preferred men teachers in an all-boys school—and this time he was sure he was safe by specifying that the math teacher be an engineer. Imagine his surprise when this five-foot miss, complete with picture hat at a dashing angle, walked in to apply for the job. He was speechless. But Isabel got the job. Later, she became the first teacher of aviation theory in the New York City high schools.

The *real* Isabel Ebel, however, still scoured the country every vacation, hoping someone might need an aeronautical engineer enough to be willing to give a woman a chance to prove what she could do. She made a 200,000-mile circuit of every aircraft plant in the country, looking for a way into aviation.

"Every summer I'd get in my car and drive around, looking for a job helping to build planes. In 1936 I sat down and wrote a letter of application to every aircraft company in the United States. There were no openings, some didn't reply at all and others merely sent form letters."

This circuit of the country finally brought her to the doors of the Northrup Aircraft Company in California, where she was given a job in their engineering division. It looked for a while as if now she were finally on the inside, but three months later, without warning, a strike and sell-out of the company sent her back to New York to start all over again.

Back to teaching once again, Isabel decided that an aeronautical engineer really should know something of the fundamentals of flight for herself, so she started taking flying lessons. Before long she had her private license, was well on her way to a commercial, and with a third-class radio license was making cross-country trips on the beam.

She tells a joke on herself about the first acquaintance with two-way radios some years ago:

"Coming down after a flight with a friend, who had just finished a long conversation on his two-way radio, I very naively queried, 'Who's your friend Roger?'"

And that from the only full-fledged woman aeronautical engineer in the country! Perhaps it is this ability to laugh at herself plus unusual poise and a gift for quick repartee that enables Isabel to hold her own in any group.

By 1939 with half the world at war and the other half preparing for it, aircraft production gained impetus rapidly in the United States and trained engineers were at a premium. Now at last women were being given opportunities to show what they could do in engineering. Isabel Ebel was given her first real engineering position by the Grumman Aircraft Engineering Corporation.

There, as the first woman in the engineering department, she did a bit of everything, trying to find where she would fit in best. She read blueprints and did some drafting, quite a bit of stress analysis on engine mounts and wing ribs, complicated mathematical calculations on the strength of various airplane parts, and even some original work on a design for a retractable pilot tube. She spent much of her time at Grumman doing wing testing on the XF 5-1, an experimental twin-engined Navy fighter.

Her two years at Grumman were a valuable experience for the company as well as Miss Ebel.

"There is no doubt that she broke the ice for the many women we now employ in our engineering department," one Grumman official said, "although even today, with women comprising 25 per cent of that department's personnel, there is no one with Miss Ebel's qualifications. Unfortunately for her, she was a real pioneer, ten years ahead of her time, and Grumman just wasn't ready for her. Today, or even two or three years ago when we took in our first group of women engineering aides and draftsman, she would have found it much easier."

One difficulty that this capable young woman faced at Grumman was a lack of the conversational background in engineering that most boys grow up with. She had the knowledge and the ability but naturally was at a loss with men who had talked engineering and worked with mechanical contraptions since grammar-school days, and had been in the engineering field for years.

"Pioneers always have a tough time of it," one of the engineers with whom she worked commented, "perhaps because they feel such a terrific responsibility for others who will follow them. Isabel had plenty of determination as well as ability. I can tell you one amusing incident quite aside from her work, to prove it.

"She and I were riding our horses through the woods one day, when we came to a stream. Isabel didn't realize that her hired horse, Rifle, was a 'mud-turtle'—the type of animal that lies down in any water which is above his fetlocks. As we reached the middle of the stream, Rifle very neatly rolled over on his back, nearly pinning Isabel beneath him. She jumped off quickly, walked to the bank, and cut a switch, and then, looking

Rifle firmly in the eye, said 'Now let's try it again!'
Maybe it was the tone in her voice—anyway, this time
he crossed the stream without hesitation."

After she had been at Grumman two years, Brewster
Aeronautical offered her a more responsible job, which
she accepted. In charge of Brewster's development and
new design department, it looked as if Isabel were all
set. But no, when she had been there only a few
months, the department was dissolved—change of company policy or something, and Isabel moved on to a
job with Snead and Company in New Jersey.

"At Snead we were building a large transport glider
for the navy," she says, "and my group had to prepare
all the aerodynamic stress-analysis reports for the project." By this time she had seven men working under
her—quite a step upward for a girl who a few years
before had had trouble getting a foothold in engineering.

Isabel liked the work at Snead but was dissatisfied
with the organization of the aeronautical division. She
decided to leave after a few months. Evidently the
company itself agreed with her dissatisfaction because,
shortly after she left, the aeronautical division was dissolved.

The war was probably the greatest factor in the
breakdown of the wall against women in aeronautical
engineering. It created a demand for aeronautical engineers and the existing male supply was not nearly
sufficient to meet the demands.

Isabel was particularly pleased to get into a field that
would continue to expand after the war, which might
not be true of jobs in aircraft factories handling war
contracts. Isabel Ebel believes that there is a very def-

inite future for women in the air-line companies since women have shown that with adequate training they can do a majority of air-line jobs as well as men.

The work Isabel is doing at present for United Air Lines involves much less structural design than any of her previous positions; it consists more of aerodynamic and economic study.

"Sometimes my assistant and I spend weeks on one airplane plan, making hypothetical changes in interior arrangements, engine, or ventilating system—putting the plane through an analytical mill to see what such changes will do to operation. We run into unconventional designs occasionally also—jet-propelled planes, helicopters, and flying wings," she adds. Flying wings in particular have always interested her, since as a student at N.Y.U. she designed such a model for her advanced degree.

The end of the war has not brought any great changes in the airplanes used by the air lines, Isabel believes. Undoubtedly converted military planes will be used wherever possible for a while; and, as in time these ships become obsolete and greater scientific advancements in engine development, airplane structure, and aerodynamic design are made, new air transports will appear.

Today in the mock-up shop, Isabel and other United engineers are working out problems of future plane design, many of which are still military secrets. It won't do any harm to tell you though that most recently she has been working on plans to reorganize and simplify the instrument boards of large aircraft.

"One of the most interesting aspects of my work is the opportunity to hear about investigations being made and possibilities considered for future domestic air-line use."

Isabel says that she has found men and women about equal in ability when they have equal background of training and experience, and one as easy to work with as another.

"The fact that I am a woman has never hindered me with any engineering work I have done, but I don't know that it has given me any particular advantage either. From my own experience and observations, I do not believe that men or women have any inherent qualities that specifically fit them for engineering or any similar scientific work.

"If there are professional attributes due to the sex of an individual, I have never noticed them. Of course, I really have no right to draw conclusions because none of the comparatively few women with whom I have come in contact in engineering have had a chance to secure as much training or experience as I have had." This was not a field that can be built up quickly, since it required a minimum of four years schooling.

"I hope that the return to peacetime production will not adversely affect the so-called 'open field' in engineering for women. United Air Lines I know does not anticipate any great personnel turnover just because the war is over, but we do expect to expand. There will probably always be some men who will resent the invasion of women into the engineering profession, but I have found on the whole that once the original barrier is down, women are fairly well accepted."

PAULINE GOWER

LOIS COOTS TONKIN

NANCY LOVE *(center)*

MAXINE MILES *(center)*

ELLEN CHURCH RECEIVES THE AIR MEDAL FROM
LIEUTENANT GENERAL BRERETON

HELEN HARRISON

J. T. Walters

CAROLINE IVERSON ON THE WAY TO GREENLAND

ETHEL COLWELL

VALENTINA GRIZODUBOVA

Helen Montgomery

Brown Brothers

Phoebe Omlie

ISABEL EBEL